APPALACHIAN
REVIEW

VOL. 51, NO. 4
FALL 2023

50 YEARS OF
TRADITION. DIVERSITY. CHANGE.

EDITOR
Jason Kyle Howard

STUDENT ASSISTANTS
Lie Ford
Paula Keshdarian

MANUSCRIPT READERS
Katherine Scott Crawford
Patti Frye Meredith

ADVISORY BOARD

Richard Hague
Marc Harshman
Maurice Manning
Karen Salyer McElmurray

Lee Smith
Lyrae Van Clief-Stefanon
Neela Vaswani
Crystal Wilkinson

ESTABLISHED IN 1973
PUBLISHED QUARTERLY
by Berea College
www.appalachianreview.net

Electronic submissions only at www.appalachianreview.net. Distributed through a partnership between the University of North Carolina Press and Duke University Press. Basic subscription price: $32/year for individuals, $62/year for institutions. For subscription requests and inquiries, visit the magazine's website, email subscriptions@dukepress.edu, or call 888-651-0122 (toll-free in the US and Canada) or 919-688-5134.

CONTENTS

INTERVIEW

COVER PHOTOGRAPH
Carey Neal Gough

EDITOR'S NOTE

JASON KYLE HOWARD

A few weeks ago I spoke with Monic Ductan, whose recently released debut short story collection *Daughters of Muscadine* is garnering attention and acclaim. Our conversation is featured in this issue, and it illustrates why she is one of Appalachia's most promising writers. As we spoke, Ductan explained how Dorothy Allison has influenced her writing. She proclaimed Allison's *Bastard Out of Carolina* as "probably my favorite novel."

"I come from a family similar to hers," Ductan observed, "and I want to tell my family's stories, even though they may not always be pleasant to read about."

For many writers, this belief is foundational, one of the primary reasons we write. Now, more than ever, we need the stories of Affrilachians, Appalatins and Appalasians; of LGBTQ+ Appalachians; of immigrants; of women and men whose voices have been overlooked or even dismissed outright.

Sometimes, as the poet AE Hines writes in "Bed," people might despair at what he calls an "obsession with the darkness" and call for happier stories. Gentle narratives that provide escape and don't make too many demands of the reader. Those are valuable and necessary in their own right, and they are certainly part of my own reading life. But also vital to our region and country—to our souls—are the stories that confront the darkness without blinking and help us sort through the questions we carry, some of which we may not even realize we hold.

As editor, I hope this magazine makes room for those queries and stories. I believe they are certainly alive and well in the pages of this issue. A story about deep grief. An essay that questions our notions of progress and development. Poems about disappearance, aging, seeing Prague in the early hours and fly fishermen who "chase the sun."

When I asked Ductan what advice she might have for young writers, she encouraged them to look any fears and anxieties they might have in the face and "not...be afraid to tell the story they want to tell."

"I think sometimes the best writing comes from people who just go for it," she said. "Writers like Tennessee Williams, Salman Rushdie and Toni Morrison knew that not everyone would be receptive to their work, and yet they wrote it anyway. To me, that's brave." ■

MY GRANDMOTHER'S HOUSE

DEAN MARSHALL TUCK

When dad was young, walking his coon dog in the woods near the old home, he heard a woman's voice call his name. He was certain it wasn't his imagination because the dog reared its head and turned in the direction the sound came from. He ran from the woods, across the field, up the porch and into the home to find Grandma speaking with a friend in the living room. Catching his breath, he asked what she wanted. Grandma and Mrs. Alice gave a perplexed look and assured him neither had called him.

■ ■ ■

My great-grandmother was either a witty, sharp woman or a domineering bully depending on who you ask. The latter response you would most likely receive from her daughter-in-law, Grandma. My great-grandmother lived in the old home with Grandaddy and Grandma, and their three children until she died. When my aunt was a child, some nights after she had gone to bed, this woman would slip into her room and stand over her, watching her sleep. Grandma warned her to stop: "If she wakes up in the night to find some stringy-white-haired, gray-faced old hag looking down at her, you'd scare her to death!" When she failed to comply, Grandma began locking my aunt in the bedroom—all the interior rooms still had locks with skeleton keys. Later, my great-grandmother made it clear she was not threatened by Grandma's presence, nor her position in the house. She struck her fist into her cupped palm one day, sitting at the kitchen table, but Grandma, irrepressible Grandma, looked her dead in the eyes and said, "Woman, if you threaten me in *my* house again, I will drop your ass on the floor."

■ ■ ■

In his teen years, dad was plagued by a recurring dream: he's on the slate roof of the old home, patching some shingles with Granddaddy when suddenly he loses his footing and begins to slide down the steep pitch—always on the same side of the house where there would be no chance of catching himself, nothing to grab onto to stop his sliding—and falling over the eaves, but he wakes from the dream in terror each time before he hits the ground. When dad finally has enough of the dream, he gets a ladder and climbs on top of the house. He walks across the roof to the side where he always falls in the dream. He carefully scoots himself down in a crouching position to the edge and, like a cat, surveys the distance a beat, and jumps right off the house, a good fourteen-feet drop. Being a pretty agile and limber young man, he has no problem navigating the landing, just a sore wrist for a few days, but he never has the dream again.

■ ■ ■

My great-grandmother, in her hurry across the living room, trips over an ottoman and breaks her hip. She's taken to the hospital and never comes home again. A generation later, Granddaddy dies of cancer not long after I am born. While everyone else opened Christmas presents in Grandma's living room, I'm told I laid on his chest in the next room, wailing.

■ ■ ■

On vacation from Rock Island Arsenal, my dad's brother sleeps in the room where the old woman would watch his sister sleep. Lying on the bed, facing the wall, he feels his wife lie down beside him, her body pressing against him. Half-dozing, he speaks to her, but she doesn't reply. Before he can fall asleep, he hears his wife call his name from the living room, asking if he would like a glass of water. He turns over to find he's been alone all this time. He never sleeps in the old home again, opting for hotels in the nearest city.

■ ■ ■

One day after school, I'm watching cartoons alone in the kitchen. The emergency broadcast system's strange electric buzzer takes hold of me. I cut off the television. I run to the living room and Grandma's recliner is empty. The buzzer blares on her television, a distorted voice garbled in the speakers. I kill hers, too. The house is quieter than I can ever recall. I dash to the front porch where the swing and the rockers are gently swaying. It is late afternoon, and the trees are a sick pale green, the skies are lavender, and the corn barn and buildings across the road are like ashes. I have seen the world look this way before tornados and hurricanes. There's a balminess in the air, but a beading cold sweat brings with it a feverish chill. I call for

The emergency broadcast system's strange electric buzzer takes hold of me. I cut off the television. I run to the living room and Grandma's recliner is empty.

Grandma in every room in the old home—even the ones I'm too scared to linger in—before diving beneath my aunt's old bed. In church, they say when Jesus comes back, it'll be just like this. No man knows the hour. Two in a field, one left behind. I remain under the bed until dad returns with Grandma from the tobacco barns.

■ ■ ■

Back behind the house, across from the fields, a path follows the woods down to the end of the property. Dad has found the bleached skull of a deer, a young buck with short cow-horn antlers. At a bend in the path, dad lodges the horned skull in the branch of a dogwood tree. There it stays for months where it becomes a kind of sight marker, gleaming white bone in the dark of the dogwood's green. Then one autumn day, on our way back to fish the pond, we ride by only to find the skull missing. We get out and kick around the fallen leaves near the tree, and the toe of dad's boot finds something solid. He clears away the leaves, but it's not a skull: it's a large, empty jar like the kind that might be filled with whole pickles, sitting on a general store counter by the cashier clerk. The lid-less jar is empty and perfectly clean. A trade.

■ ■ ■

Grandma's well turns bad. A neighbor wearing a pith helmet comes to the house with several divining rods. Some he has more luck with than others. He trains each of us and gives us a few. We hide them behind our backs when cars drive by. Later, the man who digs the well says, "Don't matter where you dig, you're gonna find water." My dad says, "Yeah, but we're paying by the foot ain't we?"

■ ■ ■

My grandmother wakes up one day with cloudy vision. She loses her sight completely within twenty-four hours. She will not live to see the anniversary of this day. Not long after her funeral, my aunt and my dad sit quietly in the living room, thinking about this final year of providing round-the-clock care for her, but saying very little. Across the room on the old wooden stereo are rows of framed pictures of us all: me, my sister, my family, the Iowans, Granddaddy, Grandma... Two pictures clatter, face-forward, seemingly of their own volition. "Damn, Mama. Lived here your whole life. Can't you walk around the house without bumping into your own furniture?" my dad says. They walk to the stereo to right the pictures, both of my grandmother: one, she's a teenager sitting on a bicycle, her hair is long and dark, a distant look, the ghost of a smile—"I won't so bad looking, was I?" she once said to me, showing me the picture. "Someone should have told me."—and the other, a church directory portrait of the woman I knew.

■ ■ ■

My dad and I are fishing at the bank of the pond through the woods behind grandma's house—my aunt lives there now. We've caught very little. The setting sun is shimmering out where we're casting our lines. For a moment, we stop and look along the bank to our right. There, just this side of a willow oak tree, is the subtle movement of a creature with the gaping maw of a fish larger than any he or I have ever caught, a blurry, brown body, and two fur-covered arms that end with claws, but as soon as our peripheral vision can touch the creature, it sloughs quietly into the water, never to be seen again. We describe to each other what we saw—both the same thing—but words won't untangle the image of this backwater chimera.

■ ■ ■

My aunt's husband has seen many strange things I am inclined not to believe. It is difficult to accept the experiences of those who do not see as we see. Sitting by the window where my grandmother sat each day for so many years before her vision failed, he sees in the driveway a dark beast on all fours. Red glowing eyes look back at him. "Its hide is darker than black," he says, "like staring into a hole, and the longer you look, it's like the hole is opening inside you, inside your ribcage, behind your heart." He says when the beast stands to its full height, "the emptiness stands with him." The beast turns its gaze and moves on, and so my aunt's husband believes death will not come for him and smokes another cigarette.

■ ■ ■

One quiet afternoon, my aunt talks with me over lunch while my daughter sleeps in her crib. She says, "Your father wouldn't tell you this—you and your sister were children at the time—but one time he saw a woman dressed in white standing near the grapevines behind the house, beneath the old apple tree. Don't tell him I told you," she says. She has lived in my grandmother's house many years now. She tells me story after story—a phantom hand knocking on the front door's stained glass; a man in faded green work pants and shirt walking across the long front porch, one end to the other, before disappearing; firm shoulder taps she receives when she sitting in Grandma's seat by the window; the sounds of ceiling beams, rafters crashing down in the attic waking her in the night—and it's all too much to take, really.

■ ■ ■

My dad and I are fishing on the beaver pond behind the old home. In the small aluminum jon boat, we watch the sunlight fading all around us. We've caught many small fish and a few bass and returned them to the pond. We've seen heron, geese, ducks, a woodpecker, osprey, and crows. We are talking softly when a loud, guttural call comes from deep in the woods. Perhaps if a goat were the size of a horse and had the lung capacity of a giant man, this might mimic the sound we heard. Offering my best version of the call, I return the sound in the direction of its origin. It responds in similar fashion. "Do it again," dad says. The thing returns my call many times, but each time we hear its reply, it seems to come from a different part of the woods. By now, it is dark. We paddle back to the bank and take our gear to the truck like always. Tacit decisions are made concerning when, if ever, to speak of this thing again.

■ ■ ■

A week later, we return to the beaver pond, jesting to each other about the thing we heard. Only a week ago and it already feels like a memory or a peculiar dream. We fish and catch nothing. "Call it one more time," dad says. I do. Before I can draw my next breath to remark how silly this all was, the thing howls back from the depths of the forest. But the water is cold and our paddles slog through the grassy shallows, the hull hangs on great tree roots reaching up like withered hands from the murky bottom, and it is too near dark for any such foolishness. ■

ORPAH

Am I bitter?

What kind of question is that
even

I know what
you want me to say

That's enough

I have screamed my share into the heavens
they look and sound the same here
you know like we all haven't lost

like we all haven't wanted

to go back.

LUCAS WARREN

MILLIE RECALLS A SUNDAY AFTERNOON

Front porch, late July, 1917.
Millie and her mother snap beans for supper.
Her brother plucks his banjo,
circling a song in fits and starts.

Millie tunes into the cicadas,
tunes out the dropped notes.
Her father swings, the rusted chain
keeping time. He coughs

as if about to say something
but never does. Below, hydrangeas
toss up their blue puffs.
Why does Millie return

again and again to this moment?
Sunlight wobbles through the pin oak leaves.

CARRIE GREEN

MILLIE ERASES HER CASE NOTES (INFLUENZA, 1918)

Open my eyes to find

      the   future   clanging
      into

                  the   margins.

the sun   burns white   overexposed

all the color leached out

I had a little bird, its name was Enza.
I opened the window, and in flew Enza.

my chest rattles its wings.

eyes rimmed with shadows.

what remains

my brother's   letters

19

NOTES ON DISAPPEARANCE

Dawn unravels a swath of pink across the fields.
No signs, no clues on the morning of the disappearance.

A banjo's tinny plink, a note caught in the throat—
fragments that haunt us after a disappearance.

Sun-bleached, the hills fade to sepia. The ashman gathers
hours on the afternoon of the disappearance.

In dreams ordinary as laundry in sun, the missing return.
We wake to the nightmare of disappearance.

The clouds obscure the moon like gauze. But witness
the plague of stars on the night of the disappearance.

Carrot Top, Freckle Face, Mildred Ann. I long to hear
my brother tease again, those hated names another disappearance.

CARRIE GREEN

SOUTH
CAROLINIAN
JUNGLE

JOSEPH VICKERY

We drove across roads that allowed the landscape to determine their path rather than the ingenuity of engineers. Faded-grey lanes clung to the curved, undulating earth like kudzu; vague lines between the asphalt and rocky soil blended together within the mottled, sporadic shadows of trees. Deer, frozen and complacent, would sometimes peek out from the tree line waiting to cross—more cautious than the less fortunate rabbits and opossums. Grain silos that were one cracked brick away from collapsing, stood defiantly next to their modern steel cousins. The closer we got, the more often we would come across one-lane bridges barely able to hold themselves up as we rolled along over creeks, streams, and the occasional overachieving rivulet. My mom, God bless her, suffered in silence with road sickness as I treated our 1990 Astro Van like a rally car—I was only fifteen and my dad let me take the wheel despite only having a driver's permit and not being able to legally drive outside of Tennessee. But my mind was elsewhere: I was fixated on what was to be my last excursion through my very own "Jungle Trail."

The destination for everyone else, however, was my aunt's wedding that was to take place in the back yard of my grandparents' house the following day. The "Homeplace," as everyone called it, stood tall and proud above everything else ever since it was built in the early fifties. The driveway was nearly a quarter-of-a-mile long and rose and fell like waves carved from the very granite the house stood upon. The driveway was nearly enveloped by a tunnel of sentry-like pine trees that reached down with limbs heavy with age, tapping at the car's roof as I drove forward. The needle-covered, auburn ground stood in stark contrast to the unflinching green above. The pines eventually opened up to reveal a fleet of Lincoln Continentals all built between the late seventies and mid-eighties. Canary yellow, slate gray, and titanium white were but a few of the colors represented in my family's then-obsession with the make and model. Each boat-on-wheels had carved out a spot on the dry, sandy soil—a mosaic of colors both above and below. The view from the back yard was idyllic, post-card worthy even, with Table Rock

Mountain shining with reddish-orange light in the setting sun; it had the appearance of a hazy painting you could actually enter and explore. The horse pasture in the background gently sloped downward as though politely moving out of the way of the view. I could smell the pleasantly pungent smell of figs that had fallen too soon from the fig tree that hugged the house.

Sunday, my grandparents' sixteen-year-old shaggy mut, found abandoned as a puppy, affected a sort of half-shuffle, half-hop to greet us. My grandmother would soon follow, ready to dole out hugs and kisses too genuine and loving to ever forget. My dad's sisters nearly fell out the door as they hopped onto the red brick patio mid-dance while wearing wooden clogs. (They were prone to clog dance just about anywhere. From buffet restaurants, to airports, to movie theaters, no place seemed off limits. No one knows when or how the tradition started, but I like to think that uncertainty only adds to the allure.) Once the din of overly enthusiastic greetings and ground-rattling dancing settled to a more manageable pitch, we all filed inside to the kitchen full of freshly made grits, biscuits, and stone gravy. With each subsequent wave of the screen door, the hint of bacon grease and salted pork wafted from inside. I lingered for a few seconds as I looked back, out toward the Jungle Trail that awaited me the next morning. But first, the "Pine Cone Convention."

Every time my family and I made the twelve-hour-long drive to visit my grandparents, my grandfather would celebrate our arrival that night with a dangerously large bonfire. He would spend the entire week before we arrived gathering up many pounds' worth of pine cones and needles that had fallen along the driveway. He stuffed every last one into paper grocery bags he had saved for that very purpose, then tossed the bags into a four-foot-tall brick chimney-like structure that sat next to the gate to the horse pasture. Ever since I was five years old, my grandfather started to let my cousins, older brother, and me fight over who got to light the fire. After drenching the cones and needles with an entire bottle of lighter fluid, my grandfather would save a few drops to put on a single pine cone and hand it to whoever made the best argument for the honor. Like the Olympic Torch, the victor would hold the flaming cone high as some sort of offering to the gods, then toss it into the diminutive, makeshift chimney. Despite knowing it was coming, the whoosh of hot air and crackling sap scared me every time.

But a decade later, I wasn't too keen on fighting for the honor. Instead, I stared into the night, past the swirling flames that fought to distract me from the adventure I had looked forward to ever since we received my aunt's wedding invitation in the mail.

■ ■ ■

I woke up at five a.m. the next morning. My dad and grandfather were the only other people awake at the time; they were reclined in wrought-iron chairs on the back porch, drinking coffee and eating watermelon. I silently joined them as they continued their conversation.

I glanced at the corner where a dozen walking sticks leaned against the wall. My dad must have seen this because he told me, "In due time, son; not until I finish my coffee."

"Not until I finish my coffee." That seemingly innocuous phrase haunted my brother and me growing up. Depending on what we had asked for, finishing his coffee could last five minutes, or it could mysteriously last all day. Our dad's coffee mug had the ability to become truly bottomless if he wanted it to. Nonetheless, I sheepishly asked, "We'll have time before the wedding, right?" My dad simply smiled and offered me some coffee despite knowing I hated the stuff.

Eventually, my dad gave in and told me to round up everyone who wanted to join. Since, however, everyone else in the family were definitely not morning people, he knew I'd have to sulk just a little longer. But eventually everyone else did wake up and all but my grandmother joined. All-in-all, there were twelve of us ready for one last excursion.

After everyone had chosen their favorite walking stick, my grandfather walked outside with his usual bombastic, jovial flair that so often prompted new people he met to ask what church he preached at. As always, he was wearing his hunter

Everyone played their part and bowed theatrically as he led the way to the horse pasture. The smell of charred pine cones still lingered that morning...

green windbreaker that he had custom embroidered on the back in bright yellow letters: "Trail Boss." Everyone played their part and bowed theatrically as he led the way to the horse pasture. The smell of charred pine cones still lingered that morning, fighting to overpower the smell of well-fed horses.

I was on watermelon duty that morning. I held a platter of watermelon rinds in one hand and a walking stick in the other as we approached the pasture gate. Even the Trail Boss waited for me before entering, for the most ornery, ill-minded horse for three counties all around lived in that pasture. Like a feral horse chomping at the bit, the iridescent, pale-yellow mare, Lightning, appeared out of nowhere as though she'd manifested from the very soil. She was snapping her teeth and raking at the ground with her hooves. She slung her head up and down like a jackhammer. Years of dealing with Lightning had taught us to remain still as statues, that is, except for the person on watermelon duty.

I held the platter high as I slowly approached. Lightning momentarily stopped; the look in her eyes told you she was fighting between two primal urges: to protect her territory and to eat anything other than muddy grass. Once she caught the scent—and while everyone else continued to remain still—I walked along the barbed-wire fence with the platter still held high above my head. Lightning cautiously followed until I was about fifty feet away from the gate. I slid the platter under the fence and quickly, yet gingerly, hustled back to the gate.

As a singular, silent mob, we nearly jogged through the slopping pasture, past the dilapidated barn with hints of red paint hiding under the eaves, and over the dried-up creek bed until we reached the forest's edge. The forty-plus acre patch of forest was almost completely enclosed with a barbed-wire fence over a century old. In many places, the trees had grown right on top of the wire, giving the appearance of the wires going straight through the trunks. The only way inside, was a towering maple that had split at the base into two separate trunks that managed to connect back together some six feet up, leaving an oval-shaped hole just big enough to squeeze through.

I glanced back at Lightning who was stomping her way toward us having finished her bribe. I ignored the danger and let everyone else enter as I took my last look at the sign nailed to the maple's trunk that read: "Jungle Trail." One rubber snake, one wooden owl, and one plastic dinosaur were nailed onto the sign for unknown reasons.

I was the last to squeeze through the entrance that day. My aunts were taking dozens of pictures while my grandfather was already many yards ahead. Decades of traversing the Jungle Trail had compacted the sandy soil to something hard as concrete. Sunday was already there, rolling in some fallen leaves. No one ever saw Sunday leave the house, but she managed to beat us there.

Too anxious to wait, I began scouring the ground for interesting-looking rocks to add to my collection back home. I was so distracted with my head down, that I bumped right into my brother. He gave me the "gentle" tap on my shoulder that all older brothers learn at an early age, then pointed up.

It was a long-standing tradition that whoever spotted the first dead tree must attempt to push it over. If you failed, you had the choice of dancing a jig or buying everyone dinner—no one ever bought dinner. My brother didn't have to dance that day, however, as the fifty-foot-tall rotten oak tumbled with ease amid cheers from the audience.

Without so much as a peep, the Trail Boss waved his stick and headed off. In a single-file line, we followed my grandfather down past the abandoned still, through the tunnel made of fallen branches (also adorned with many rubber snakes and plastic dinosaurs), over the creek "bridge" that was nothing more than a fallen tree, until we reached the next highlight of the Jungle Trail: "Niagara." The name made sense when I was a small child since everything at that age seems more grandiose than it actually is. But at fifteen, I came to realize the name was somewhat sarcastic. Regardless, it was still one of my favorite parts. The creek had graduated to a stream by this point, and spilled over an exposed granite slab some ten feet down to a pool no bigger than most kitchens.

Whether you needed it or not, my grandfather always insisted everyone take off their shoes and soak their feet in the cool mountain water. He made the same comment about nature's beauty every time at the rest stop—something along the lines of: "Monet's got nothing on God"—but somehow it never felt dull or insincere. After a few minutes of everyone struggling to pull socks over their wet feet, we headed off once more.

The stream curved sharply and we had to cross via half a dozen boulders my grandfather placed there many years ago. As a kid, it felt like leaping between mountain tops, but as a fully-grown teenager it was little more than a wide step.

My aunts kept taking pictures; my brother kept pushing over rotten trees, my dad kept teasing my aunts for taking so many pictures; my cousins kept chasing Sunday through the

He made the same comment about nature's beauty every time at the rest stop—something along the lines of: "Monet's got nothing on God"—but somehow it never felt dull or insincere.

brush; and yet, my grandfather kept pushing forward like a man on a mission. Before we knew it, we were nearly at the end. But we still had one last stop.

Before I was born, my grandfather had found the perfect spot to have lunch. He sectioned-off a patch of forest and selectively chopped down several trees until a circle of stumps remained. Though they broke off not long after, I have vague memories of how he nailed sections of bark to each stump, giving it the appearance of a chair. My grandfather liked to claim the firewood he collected that day lasted almost a decade; in truth, he sold most of it.

As we all sat down to eat our cold sandwiches and warm water, I barely ate. I decided to spend my time observing every little detail, every little smell, sound, and sight for fear of losing the Jungle Trail forever. I heard the squirrels angrily chirping; I smelled the conifers' sap seeping to the ground; I felt the crumbling stump I sat upon; and I gazed at the smile on my grandfather's face as he sat on his wooden throne, enjoying an overripe fig. I kept searching all around, for I knew what fate awaited the forty acres of "jungle" hiding in the northwest corner of South Carolina. My grandfather spent the entire time reminiscing on past excursions while occasionally reciting scriptures he felt fit the mood and land. I had hoped his last sermon in the jungle would have lasted longer if for no other reason to hang on the childhood nostalgia just a little longer. But all things must end…all things must become memories.

We exited the Jungle Trail through the same bifurcated tree we entered. Lightning was too distracted chasing Sunday, letting us make it safely back and through the gate. I grabbed the empty platter, sticky with watermelon juice and horse saliva, and headed inside the Homeplace.

■ ■ ■

My aunt's wedding was…well, it was a wedding: a few songs, some scriptures, the exchanging of vows, then handfuls of rice getting inside your clothes.

After all the guest had left—and my aunt and her freshly-minted husband were already on the red-eye flight to Hawaii—the rest of the family lounged in the living room next to the fireplace. As he was prone to do, my grandfather had used a log way too big to fit into the fireplace (sometimes he would make the dubious claim it came from his decades-old clearing). It may have been the middle of July, but he always felt special occasions required warm fires. Looking back, his love of fires may have been less idiosyncratic and more problematic. Either way, it was who he was meant to be.

But as everyone else talked about the wedding, I was busy reliving the last time I had walked the Jungle Trail. I was sad, yet content. I didn't even mind the rattan rocking chair full of ancient baby dolls that sat in the corner. All I cared about was converting every moment into memories.

■ ■ ■

It was about two months later that my grandfather called us. He described in great detail how he walked the Jungle Trail alone, collecting all the rubber animals and hand-painted signs along the trail. He complained of the screeching of tractor treads and rumbling of diesel engines as the land was stripped clean of all its life and memories. Some might call it progress, but I would call it just another cookie-cutter housing development.

For many years, I didn't understand why my grandparents would ever sell the land they cherished. My dad was always vague in his answers when I asked why, but my mom was a little more forthcoming. I was in my twenties before she finally told me that my grandparents had fallen on hard times and needed the money to avoid the bank foreclosing on their house. After she told me why, I felt a mix of relief, understanding, and guilt for being somewhat resentful about them selling the land. But in the end, I have nothing but fond memories of the Jungle Trail and all its wonders. To most, if not all, people outside of our family, the Jungle Trail appeared to be nothing more than a goat path meandering its way through a stereotypical forest. They may scoff at the tacky decorations and exaggerated names, but none of that matters. What *does* matter is that it existed...and still exists, even if only in my memories. ■

CAROUSEL

This spring wind is
a carousel: though
it does not turn, it
still delivers me
nowhere. I would
lubricate its grating
into silence. Even
the strong-winged
herons have given
up, not stoic in the
lazy golden grass—
no, defeated, unflying,
tethered to the earth
like I am. We are
both buzzing with
the static of an element
we would rather unsee,
the bending trees
our allies until we can
step from this ride
into a day with
nothing but the sun
at our backs.

JAD JOSEY

MIRACLE LEMONADE

My grandmother, wild with God, digs holes
behind the house where her husband's sins
burrow in the wood planks.
She wears her hair like unclipped shrubs,
                    layered in wilderness.

A small graveyard surrounds her in the forest.
Bare feet in the weeds she traces letters down
her forearms with the clay stuck to her hands
from her digs. Birds twittle above her. They begin
their stock trades with broomstick straw and garland strings.

Lain before her are the plush toys she took
from my young father and his siblings,
false idols awaiting their final kiss and a thick blanket of red clay.

She baptizes each of them with lemonade and sugar crust,
prays to God to turn the liquid into holy oil before taking a knife

to the blue and pink seams of their chests.
     Then webs of thread loosen in every limb.

She stuffs each one with a quartz crystal before burying them.

Holy heart,
     holy dirt,
          holy finger tracing a cross.

My grandfather's voice whips through the tree line;

                    You out there diggin' again, woman?

Holy wad of hair,
     holy cricket wing,
          holy box with a hole in the lid.

                    That doesn't sound like me, she says.

LAUREN CRAWFORD

She's done, heads into the house
to burn more rust in the oven
or serve fruit to the dust mites
like sinners waiting for water,
like God giving out a miracle.

HOW IT FEELS TO LOSE SOMEONE

Like a splinter so thin I can't see it
Slipping between my grip
Over and over I run my finger
Across my skin to check if you're still there
Like a groomer searching for ticks
Or a wasp stinger lodged in a child's thigh
After giving up for some time
I'll forget until I sit on a stool
At just the right spot
And there you are
Yet again I cannot resist
Yet again I drag my finger
Across my skin looking
For you
Looking
Everywhere.

LAUREN CRAWFORD

DOWNSTREAM

MARY CARROLL MOORE

Jenny dropped the quilt and rooted in her suitcase. She hadn't brought many clothes; the visit was arranged hurriedly. She pulled on a T-shirt and the jeans she had arrived in yesterday, thinking of her mother packing, her face flat like a cartoon on TV, her eyes sunk to mountain shadows. She'd forgotten Jenny's underwear. But Jenny's favorite sweatshirt lay neatly folded under an extra pair of sneakers. She held the sweatshirt to her face, inhaling home. A stain centered the front, dark red ketchup her brother had spilled at lunch.

Jenny picked at it with her fingernail, then tossed the sweatshirt back in the suitcase, grabbing a fleece instead.

■ ■ ■

Where her mother came from, in Minnesota, late August was still heat-bound and sultry. In the mountains, the landscape already showed signs of fall. Last week she and Ty had gathered the first red maple leaves to iron between sheets of wax paper. Ty was a careful collector. He ironed every edge of each leaf until the wax from the paper melted completely, leaving no air pockets. Jenny concentrated more on graduating the colors of leaves from tomato to crimson. On the maple by her bedroom window, two scarlet leaves waved like hands. Maybe her grandfather would let her use the ladder in the garage.

Mom has her pictures from France, Ty had said. This is ours. Jenny could almost hear his voice, a little high and thin, mischief under the surface. Her eyes watered like she had faced a sudden strong wind. She swiped at her face with the back of her sleeve and pushed her legs through the high grass along the road, knocking into the tops of tall yellow Rudbeckia. The grass was already brushed with honey-gold. Jenny squinted at it, the way her father had taught her, to catch the flash of deeper color underneath—the quality of light. Her eyes were too blurry. She swiped at them again.

Their road curved around the river. It tumbled into rapids here, different from the glassy shallows by the farm. Jenny kicked a beer bottle down toward the water, heard it bounce and shatter. Her nostrils filled with the smoke of an early woodstove in the still air. At home, her mother would be making blueberry pancakes.

In her mind, Jenny imagined Ty's hand reaching out. They would shuffle down the gravel verge, their sneakers crunching. "Stay out of the road," she'd say. But even in her mind his response was drowned out by the now-brilliant songs of the birds in the pines lining the river.

■ ■ ■

When she got back to the house, her grandfather was up.

"Did you see the boxcars?" He was setting the table for breakfast with knives and the butter dish, a jar of homemade raspberry jam. A pile of toast, crisp and buttery, already sat squarely on a flowered plate. He pushed back his red Southern Rail cap and wiped his forehead. Grey hairs stuck out from under the cap, curling around his ears.

Jenny bit into a piece of toast, wiping a line of butter that ran down her chin. "I counted thirteen," she lied. She hadn't been near the station. The tracks were on the other side of the river.

"Same age as you. Today."

Jenny smiled into her plate. "Four days after Ty's," she said. When her grandfather didn't answer, she concentrated on taking the smallest possible bites of toast. "He always got a lot more presents."

Her grandmother made all their bread, so the toast was perfect, oatmeal flavor drenched with butter. Jenny took another piece and poked a hole in the center with her thumb, then ate everything but the crust. Empty on her plate, the ring of crust looked like a picture frame.

"Whatcha have in mind for fun today, birthday girl?" Her grandfather opened the oven door, releasing the rich smell of bacon.

"Press maple leaves," Jenny said. "We do it every fall. I need to borrow the ladder from the garage."

"No problemo." He ruffled Jenny's hair. "You want it, you just ask. Your Granny and I are so glad to have our favorite granddaughter to ourselves for a few days."

There was a silence while Gramps lifted slices of bacon onto a paper towel. "You holding up OK?"

"Did my mother call?"

"Not yet." Her grandfather cut a lump of butter and dropped it into the skillet. It spit and spun on the hot surface.

"Do you think they're ever going to find the body?" She didn't say Ty's body. Too much.

"Don't know, kiddo." He stood for a moment, staring at the skillet.

Jenny bent her head toward the bacon, inhaling salt and grease. Bacon was bad for teenagers. A boy in her class already had acne mapping his face. She pulled four strips from the pile, folded them into her mouth. The crisp edges cut her cheeks and scored her throat as she swallowed.

■ ■ ■

After lunch, her grandfather lifted the wooden ladder off its garage hook and held it while Jenny climbed. The sun stung her arms in a pleasant way, reminding her that it was still Indian summer; the noise of the cicadas was loud in the afternoon heat, lulling her.

Her grandfather had set up a card table for her in a corner near the ironing board. Jenny laid everything out and began to choose the leaf arrangements she wanted to press for the scrapbook. Out the living room window she could see the afternoon sun slanting across the yard. Her grandmother's flower garden was yellow and brown, dried seed pods waving in the breeze. "Do you like this leaf, or this one?" Jenny asked Ty in her mind. She imagined him squirming a little in the chair she had pulled out. He would lean over the table to choose exactly the right leaf for that page.

She worked steadily. Each leaf had to be chosen, set between wax paper, and pressed. Ty will be surprised, her mind whispered. Then, If they find Ty, our book will be waiting. She knew it was childish. A teenager wouldn't think these things. The officer from town had been clear. The body had not been recoverable. We dredged the lake for two days, Officer Jack had said. Then he said again. For two days.

He could've swum to the other shore, then? her mother had whispered.

Her father made a motion with both hands like he was throwing something across the room. Ty can't swim. Her mother had flinched at the hammer stroke of his voice.

She centered each leaf on its own piece of waxed paper. Every curling edge set straight was one more talisman.

Her grandmother came back to the house at five o'clock. She didn't even say *Hello, Jenny*. She just set her pocketbook on the

She knew it was childish. A teenager wouldn't think these things. The officer from town had been clear. The body had not been recoverable.

hall table and motioned to Jenny's grandfather. Behind the closed swinging door to the kitchen, their voices started rumbling.

The door squeaked as her grandfather pushed it open. He was always saying a person should oil door hinges regularly. Jenny looked up, thinking she'd remind him. But his face was tight. He walked across the room and sat down in the wicker chair she had pulled out for Ty.

"Jenny," he said. There was a pause. Jenny concentrated on arranging two crimson leaves. They had almost identical green streaks along each vein.

"Nice leaves you got there."

"I know. Look at these. Twins."

In the distance, the phone rang. Her grandmother answered it. The murmur of her voice filtered through to where they were sitting. Gramps shuffled a little in his seat. The clasp on his bib overalls clicked faintly, like a small coin falling on a stone. "What are you going to do with them?"

"I'm making a scrapbook. For Ty. He's helping me choose which ones go where." She hummed a little, studying the leaves spread in the light. Each was so individual, so beautiful. She thought suddenly of the trees lining the street outside, how none of these leaves would ever hang on those trees again. Her teacher had said leaves become dirt which become stones and rocks, everything recycling endlessly. Nothing is ever lost, her teacher had said.

"Michael, you need to pull yourself together for the sake of your family." Her grandmother's voice was loud, out of patience.

Her grandfather sighed. "They found it."

"Found what?" Jenny said. Her eyes fixed on two perfect red leaves, pointy at the edges, elegant and thin. Under the card table, her legs had begun to shake. She cupped her knees with both hands, holding tight. But her body was shaking too. She didn't have enough hands to put everywhere.

"Ty's body," her grandfather said. He reached over and laid his big hand on Jenny's shoulder, stilling her movement.

"I'm so sorry, Jenny. My sweet girl."

Her grandmother's eyes looked puffy as she served them dinner. Nobody spoke much. The phone rang as they were eating dessert, and it was for Jenny. Her mother was calling to tell her about the funeral. Granny was over that afternoon, she had a dress and shoes for Jenny to wear. Her mother swallowed as if this was the extent of her ability, as if her throat was too full to continue. Jenny should pack tonight, her mother finally said. She'd be coming home with them tomorrow after the service.

■ ■ ■

By the time they left for the church the next morning, the rain had stopped. The sky looked bleak, racing with clouds, and the air exhaled scents of the coming cold over Jenny's face and hair.

Her grandfather took the long route through town, winding the back streets, as if he knew they didn't need to hurry. But too soon, the truck's tires crunched on the gravel in the parking area next to the cemetery. Jenny saw her parents' Honda. Aunt Maggie's truck parked alongside other vehicles Jenny didn't recognize.

Her grandfather squeezed her hand, and they got out of the truck. The path to the grave site was freshly mown and smelled like spring. Jenny walked slowly, the stiff collar of her black velvet dress itching her neck, her black patent-leather shoes tight around her toes. It felt like someone else's neck, someone else's toes. Some girl who had lost a brother.

Ground up by the cemetery mower, a few specks of red leaves lay scattered on the path. The maple trunks were dark with yesterday's rain. Her parents stood at the top of the path, outlined against the sky, her mother's blond hair catching the light. Her father had one arm around her, the blond bright against his dark coat. Her mother extended a hand toward Jenny, pulled her in to the small circle of the three of them. They stood holding each other, then Patricia disengaged and leaned on her husband. Her face was empty.

The hole for Ty's grave was empty too, almost black with lack of sunlight. Now her grandfather came over and put his arm around Jenny, not saying anything, as the box containing her brother's body was lowered into the ground.

Her mother whimpered, huddling closer to Jenny's father. He bent to throw in a handful of dirt then gently propped up his wife as she dipped toward the ground to gather some soil. Jenny watched her mother's hand dig in the loose pile alongside the grave, the dirt pushing its way into her fingernails. The hand flung the dirt then lay limp against the side of her red raincoat.

She was next. On the dirt pile lay a leaf, almost perfect, edges slightly crisped from wind and cold, a true red. So instead of a handful of dirt, Jenny centered the leaf over the coffin and let it float down, and it landed exactly in the middle.

As they were walking down the cemetery path, Jenny caught sight of an old man standing by the sign that read "No ATV's Allowed." The man was looking at her; he held his hat in his hands, as if waiting. Jenny felt her grandfather's arm tighten across her shoulders. "I'll be goddamned," he muttered. She squinted through the misty air then broke away from her grandfather and walked toward the old man. He was wearing a red lumber jacket she recognized.

"Hello, there, young lady," Willard White said. He nodded at Jenny's grandfather who was coming up behind her. "Samuel."

"Willard," said her grandfather stonily. "What are you doing here?" He began to put his arm around Jenny again. She stepped forward, shrugging it off.

"They found my brother's body," she said to Mr. White.

He nodded. "I'm mighty sorry for your loss."

Her grandfather snorted. "You sure are friendly to this family all of a sudden."

Jenny turned and looked at him. "Granpa, I'd like to talk to Mr. White for a minute."

Her grandfather looked bewildered. He nodded. Jenny and Willard White watched him move across the grass toward the huddled group of people in black.

Jenny shoved her hands in her pockets. Last time she'd seen Willard White, he'd sat in front of three bonfires, deep in the hills, burning photographs. That was a day months before she lost her brother, when the worst thing to happen was getting lost in the woods and being rescued by a man her family hated. The White farm lay behind her grandfather's, the boundaries in dispute for generations no matter how many surveys her grandfather ordered. But that day at the bonfires, when Mr. White carefully escorted her back to the trail and sent her safely home, she knew he wasn't all that different from any of them now. He'd lost someone too.

Jenny pulled her diary out of her coat pocket. It was a small notebook with a worn blue cover. She riffled through the pages until she found the photograph of the man and his son, dressed for winter. She studied it for a moment, her eyes tracing the old-fashioned fur collar of the boy's coat, the edge of scorch on the corner. She'd found it, walking away from the fires, tucked it into her sleeve, not sure why.

"This belongs to you," she said, handing it to him. "I don't need it anymore."

Willard White took the photo in his big farmer's hand. Jenny noticed his thumbnail was black with dirt, as if he'd been digging. "Thank you," he said.

They turned and began to walk toward where the cars were parked.

"I loved Ty more than anyone in the world." Jenny heard herself say these words and blushed. Willard White would think she was a baby.

But he patted her shoulder. It was awkward, as if he hadn't touched anyone in a very long time. "I understand," he said quietly.

■ ■ ■

Jenny's bedroom hadn't been touched. It smelled stuffy. She opened the windows. She put her dirty T-shirt in the laundry hamper in the bathroom, folded the ketchup-stained sweatshirt into her bottom drawer, and lay the scrapbook and her blue notebook on the desk by the bed. Maybe she could finish tomorrow. Her mind spun out these words, but she knew she probably wouldn't.

The phone rang. Patricia answered it. Her voice floated up the stairs, indistinct. Jenny heard her mother go back to the kitchen, and the radio begin to play something, a jazz song. There was no sound from her father's studio. His door remained closed even after Patricia called them to dinner.

Dinner was hot dogs and macaroni and cheese. After Jenny passed the bowl around the table, her mother reached over and clasped her hand.

"Glad you're home, pumpkin."

Jenny heard her mother go back to the kitchen, and the radio begin to play something, a jazz song. There was no sound from her father's studio.

"Me too." Her skin flushed with the pet name, unused for years. She bent her head toward her plate, inhaling grease and cheese. She picked up one hot dog between her thumb and forefinger like a cigar and dipped the end into the pool of ketchup. Hot dogs were Ty's favorite. Jenny liked tuna better. She wondered if her mother had remembered to buy more.

"Isn't Dad eating?"

Patricia, her mouth full of hot dog, shook her head. She swallowed thickly. "Your grandfather called."

"What did he want?"

"He wondered if you'd be free tomorrow for lunch. He wants to go on a picnic."

"I guess." Jenny looked at the bowl of hot dogs. "Can I have the last one?"

Her mother nodded.

"Your grandfather said it would just be you two."

She squirted more ketchup onto her plate.

"He's coming to pick you up at ten."

Her mother wanted something. Jenny could feel it. She concentrated on evenly distributing each smear of ketchup with each bite of this last hot dog. She liked it when things ended that way.

■ ■ ■

The next morning was warm, as if the mountains eked out more Indian summer before winter. Jenny opened the passenger door of the red truck. It creaked. Her grandfather had forgotten to oil the hinges.

"Some good music for our journey?" He was wearing his favorite overalls. He reached over and turned on the radio. Bluegrass piped out, a song by a family named Carter. Ty would've liked it. Jenny made a note to tell him when they next talked, ignoring the hollow feeling inside her stomach.

They headed toward the river. The Adirondack blue sky stretched sparkling and clear. Through the cracked windshield, Jenny could see green mountains against the blue. "What did you bring for lunch?" She put her feet up on the dashboard, something her father never let her do in his car. Her red high tops were bright against the dull strip of road.

"Tuna sandwiches."

She smiled, satisfied.

"And a present for you." He gestured to the floor under her feet. She looked down at a brown paper bag. "Open it," he said.

Inside was a book. She had seen this book yesterday, in her grandfather's study. It was a scrapbook, like the one she was making for Ty.

"Did you make this?"

"Your father did. Look inside."

Inside were pages and pages of leaves. Old leaves, older than she was, but perfectly preserved under their wax paper. Green and red, yellow, even bright orange. Jenny turned the pages carefully, hearing them crinkle and rustle behind the wax. On the last page were only two, redder than her sneakers, the reddest things she owned. She held the waxy press to the sun coming in the truck window. The light passed through the leaves, outlining each vein, making the red glow like sunset.

"You can take those two out," her grandfather said.

Jenny teased a corner of the wax paper apart and picked up the two leaves. She held one up then the other. They were identical.

She looked over at her grandfather.

"Took your father and me all day to find them." He grinned. "Your grandmother thought we were nuts."

■ ■ ■

They turned off onto a dirt road that ran along the river. It was midway between where Jenny lived and where her grandfather lived, downstream on the river. Behind them were the fields of farms, the grasses of autumn moving in the wind like ocean waves. The river ran slow and wide in this section, and fishermen liked to wade in and wait for trout. Granite boulders dotted the surface, like they waited too. The light danced.

"Come down to the water, and bring those two leaves with you," her grandfather said.

She clambered down the bank and stood by the edge of the river, where it lapped a line of gravel. Her grandfather took off his shoes and his socks, rolled up the bottoms of his overalls. Jenny took off her sneakers and set them alongside his.

She hadn't seen her grandfather's legs before. He was an old person, in his sixties probably, but his legs looked like her father's, white but for a strip of brown along the ankles, a bracelet of color. His feet were long and elegant, and she realized they were like her own.

He took the twin leaves from her hands. One leaf he handed to Jenny, the other he took himself. He began to wade out into the water.

"Come on," he said, not looking back.

Jenny pulled off her socks. She didn't need to roll up anything, because her Bermuda shorts fell just above her knees. The water felt icy. Her feet sank in the soft silt, soothing between bare toes. Her grandfather reached the middle of the river, near the first of the waiting boulders. "Here's a good spot," he said.

Jenny came over beside him. The sun hot on her shoulders, she stood there for a moment in silence, listening. All around her the river talked, in the same way Ty spoke to her, a little shimmer in her mind no different from her own thoughts.

Her grandfather bent his long body down toward the water and gently laid his leaf on the surface. Jenny did the same. Their leaves floated for a moment, swirling in an eddy around their feet, then went downstream.

The pair stayed together for a while and eventually drifted gently apart. ■

MONIC DUCTAN

Monic Ductan was born and raised in north Georgia, so it's only natural that her debut short story collection, *Daughters of Muscadine*, is set in that oft-overlooked part of rural Appalachia. A fictional town with a complex history, her Muscadine is home to several generations of Black, working-class, mountain families whose women have faced discrimination, violence, estrangement and erasure. In muscular prose and with startling insight, she records their inner lives as they navigate situations both large and quotidian.

Ductan, a professor of literature and creative writing at Tennessee Tech University in Cookeville, Tennessee, makes clear in these stories that the past remains alive and is still deeply felt. The collection opener, "Black Water," centers on a haunting. The ghost is Ida Pearl Crawley, a Black woman who was lynched in the 1920s for purportedly setting fire to the home of her employer Herbert Munson, a white man who is also the father of her two children, which kills him and his family. Three generations later, "talk of Pearl is still plentiful as the mosquitoes that swirl around Harmony Shoals." The Crawley and Munson families keep a distance from one another, and yet it seems each knows the truth of their relations.

Other legends and legacies populate these pages, including a member of the local girls' basketball team, a girl in the 1950s who sees her loneliness reflected in the pages of Anne Frank's diary, and a mother who comes face-to-face with the daughter she gave up for adoption.

Ductan, a contributor to *Appalachian Review* and other magazines including *Oxford American, Shenandoah, Southeast Review, Good River Review* and more, recently chatted with editor Jason Kyle Howard about *Daughters of Muscadine*, representation of Black Appalachians and the writers who have inspired her.

■ ■ ■

JASON KYLE HOWARD: You have been published all over the place, from *Oxford American* and *Shenandoah* to

Monic Ductan

Kweli and here in *Appalachian Review,* but *Daughters of Muscadine* is your first book. How are you feeling now that it is out in the world?

MONIC DUCTAN: I'm elated. This is a group of stories I began writing as a graduate student when I was living down in Georgia, and I continued working on the project after I became an assistant professor [at Tennessee Technological University]. I was lucky enough to get a wonderful publisher, UPK [University Press of Kentucky], and I worked with great editors and a talented cover artist. I'm overall proud of the work.

JKH: You have created a fictional town in Georgia where most of these stories are set and to which all are connected. Can you talk a bit about the challenges and joys of making a collection of stories linked through a place?

MD: This collection was a joy to write because it made me reflect on my home. At times, it made me nostalgic. I was born and raised in Georgia, and my family has lived there for at least 200 years, so I'm deeply rooted in that place. I had some images in my head of places in north Georgia as I was writing. For instance, the shoals I mention in the book are based on Hurricane Shoals, near my hometown. One challenge I had is that I'm writing about the South, a place where people who look like me have been disadvantaged for so long. I obviously can't write the whole thing with nostalgia because I'm writing about some deeply disturbing things like lynching, racial prejudice, and family loss. It's hard to find the right balance between nostalgia and truth.

JKH: The stories take place over a hundred years, from the 1920s to the present. You do a beautiful job of placing us subtly in each time period. How do you go about doing that?

JKH: I enjoyed writing about the various time periods in the book. For instance, "June's Menorah" is set in 1959, so I tried to throw in some subtle references, such as the type of car they drove and the fashion of that time period. I admire vintage fashions, and I love Peter Pan collars and those A-line skirts from mid-twentieth century America. I wrote each story separately and then thought about how I could link them together. The name Crawley comes up often, and that was purposeful. I wanted to depict life in a small town where you hear some of the same surnames over and over again for generations.

JKH: You focus a great deal on the complexities of our most intimate relationships—between siblings, between parents and children, between lovers. Why are you attracted to telling these stories?

MD: I've always been inspired by the stories I enjoy reading and the media I consume. Some of my favorite stories are about family relationships and friendships. I also love strong women characters. I grew up watching *Fried Green Tomatoes* and *Norma Rae.* I also love reading books about complicated family relationships, such as *Bastard Out of Carolina,* which is probably my favorite novel.

JKH: Each of the book's stories is so well structured and include so many vivid characters and that tremendous sense of place that binds them all together. Who have been your major influences in the short story form?

MD: Where to begin? There are so many good short story writers! Here are a few stories that come to mind, and I've listed the authors, though I'm sure I'm forgetting a few stories: "The Third and Final Continent" and "Hell-Heaven" by Jhumpa Lahiri, "A Good Man is Hard to Find" by Flannery O'Connor, "Everyday Use" by Alice Walker, "Going to Meet the Man" by James Baldwin, "Home Visit" by Natalie Sypolt, "Bullet in the Brain" by Tobias Wolff.

I'm currently reading Stephanie Powell Watts's collection, *We Are Taking Only What We Need,* and I like that book a lot.

JKH: You're from northern Georgia where these stories are set. How challenging is it to write about home, or your place of origin, with honesty and complexity?

MD: When I was a child, I embraced my town because it was the only place I really felt I knew, and then as a young adult I became more critical. I grew up poor, partly because my mother and father were denied access to a good education in the Jim Crow South. Barriers to education have plagued Appalachia too, of course. Coming to that realization as a young adult turned me bitter. I started to become aware of how others view Southerners, how others view Black people, and how Appalachian people are viewed.

One thing I love about literature and about regionalist literature is its diversity. The way I write about the South and the way I write about Appalachia would look different than how you or another Appalachian writer would do it. My stories are colored by my experiences growing up poor and Black. I grew up in Appalachia, though my Black family would probably never define us as Appalachian. I've never heard my mama use the word. She'd probably see it as a government label, and she is often distrustful of government. In fact, she once asked me what "Black English" is, even though she clearly speaks it. She just sees it as "English" because it's normal to her.

Now, at middle age, I feel the need to embrace all those labels. There's nothing shameful about growing up poor, Black, Southern, and Appalachian. My writing grapples with this struggle to accept and reject labels. As a Black woman, I've often felt I couldn't be proud to be Southern because of the South's painful history, but now I'm viewing it differently. My ancestors built the South and the U.S. economy with their hands, and our influences on the Southern dialect and food are undeniable. There's pride in that.

Dorothy Allison once wrote in an essay that when she was growing up in the 1950s the poor people depicted on TV and in the media were the good poor. They were poor, but they were hard-working, clean, and other adjectives that made them respectable. Her family, Allison points out, wasn't like that. They were poor and uneducated and dirty and angry. I think overall, she's saying that her stories also deserve to be told, even though her family were not the respectable poor. I agree with her. I come from a family similar to hers, and I want to tell my family's stories, even though they may not always be pleasant to read about.

JKH: Although this is thankfully beginning to change, the presence and stories of Black Appalachians have historically been erased or minimized. What do you hope *Daughters of Muscadine* communicates about the Black Appalachian experience?

MD: One reader reached out to me on social media to say that the book made her homesick for her hometown in the South, and that was a big compliment to me. I hope I've depicted this place well enough to do it justice, and by that I mean that I want people to recognize their homeplace when they look at it. I also think representation is important. When I was a child, I read mostly white writers and felt that most of those books weren't written with me in mind. I wanted *Daughters of Muscadine* to be a book for women like me, a book in which Black women are at the center and not the margins.

JKH: Besides writing fiction, you do quite a bit of nonfiction. How are the forms different and similar for you?

MD: My nonfiction is usually narrative, so there's not always a big difference for me. I tend to write a lot about my family in nonfiction. If the story works better by sticking to the truth, then I write an essay. If I want to explore and change the details and see where it takes me, then I write a story. My essays feel a lot more personal than my stories, though. Plus, it's sometimes difficult to link my experiences together in a cohesive way, which is one big challenge I find in writing personal essays.

JKH: Any chance we'll see an essay collection in the future?

MD: Yes, I do want to publish an essay collection. I have about five to six essays I'm proud of, and so far they all fit together thematically. Most of them focus on poverty, the South, and race. I have a few essays on the backburner right now while I'm trying to finish a novel manuscript. Once the novel is complete, I'll go back to the essays. I've been trying to write about my mother for a few years now. She was born in poverty in 1939 and had a tough upbringing. I haven't figured out how to tell her story yet. I'd also like to write an essay about how I grew up in poverty in the South and how that has shaped who I became as an adult. I started a draft of it recently, but I was tackling too much, and the first draft felt scattered because there were so many ideas I wanted to force into it. I think it will become a much longer essay than I originally intended.

JKH: Are there writers in particular who have encouraged you or fostered your work?

MD: I studied writing throughout my time in academia and have been privileged to have some great teachers. Anne Sanow gave me a lot of good advice and saw the earliest drafts of some of the stories in *Daughters of Muscadine*. In workshop, she once held up a story of mine and said, "This is fine. This is good, but I don't know if I'll remember it tomorrow." It was exactly what I needed to hear about that story. She is a great reader and gives critical advice. I also studied with Alice Friman, a poet who helped me write more concise poems, and she often pointed to something in my work that I had overlooked.

John Holman, Sheri Joseph, Allen Gee, Martin Lammon, Peter Selgin, Laura Newbern, and Steven Barthelme were the other teachers I studied under. I learned something important from every one of them. For instance, John Holman and Steve Barthelme each had a way of pushing back on student opinions in workshop in a way that made us defend our opinions by pointing to specific parts of the text. This is something I try to emulate when I teach workshops.

JKH: As professors, you and I both work a lot with young writers. What advice might you have for them, and for young writers of color in particular?

MD: This sounds like simple advice, but I often tell my students to write with a purpose. When I first started writing, I knew I wanted to tell stories, but I didn't stop to think about what types of stories I wanted to tell. Now, after this first collection, I feel I know quite a bit more about what sort of writer I want to be.

I always tell students not to be afraid to tell the story they want to tell. Sometimes they're worried about what everyone will think of them, or they worry especially about what their classmates will say in workshop. I think sometimes the best writing comes from people who just go for it. Writers like Tennessee Williams, Salman Rushdie, and Toni Morrison knew that not everyone would be receptive to their work, and yet they wrote it anyway. To me, that's brave.

I always tell my students that you have to be passionate and steadfast to finish writing a book. Otherwise, you'll find a thousand reasons to not keep going. Most writers I know work day jobs and have families that take priority over everything else, so it's sometimes hard to stay motivated to write. You have setbacks in the writing, too. For instance, I must've written a hundred drafts of that last story in my collection before I was satisfied with it.

I think sometimes writers of color are discouraged when writing about race. In workshop, other writers have said things like, "[Chimamanda Ngozi] Adichie already wrote about hair, so I think you can omit that part of your story." I once told a professor that I often write about race and the working-class, and he said, "What are you going to do with that?"

He clearly thinks that everything has already been said about race and class, and maybe most of it has been said, but it won't stop me from writing my version.

I tell students that no one can choose your subject matter for you. Students sometimes get frustrated if I ask questions and don't understand all the elements of the fantasy story they've created. I tell them to ignore whatever advice isn't helpful, and focus on what *is* helpful. That's what I did in workshop. I was taught mostly by white writers who have never been poor or experienced racism, and they sometimes gave bad advice about those things. I ignored that and focused on what *was* helpful, and I still learned a lot. ■

THE FIRST TIME SHE GOES MISSING

My sister and I call out to our mother,
lost in the Carolina pines, swimming
in her own private darkness where

green needles shimmer in the soft
purple twilight, and the wind whispers
her name. This, how a child learns to pray.

Air too sweltering for sleep, in this way
a new protector, forged from a son. A man
who will lay back the darkness in spite

of his fear. Who has learned to wait
for the slow pulse of morning, for dawn
to pass again across her eyes. Even now,

I imagine her gone to the black recesses,
sinking into the loamy soils, gauzy palace
of her pale summer self. Sometimes,

late in the night, I still hear her
crying out at the brightness of the moon
as it slices through the trees.

AE HINES

BED

My husband despairs my obsession
with the darkness, wants me to write
happier poems the way he wishes
I'd make our bed when I roll out
in the morning, long after he starts his day.
I sit above a small white sea
scattering biodegradable ink across
this recycled page, but can't help thinking
of the widow next door who tells me
it's little things that piss her off now: him
not being there to make their bed together,
how each day she pulls the sheets
up around his cold pillow, then is unable
to make it through the morning paper
without him there passing her page
after page. "Bad news, anyway," she says.
Wars, pandemic, sunrise
turning her windows red. Some mornings
she stares at his photo at the edge
of her breakfast table, young and handsome,
still so brilliant, and it's enough
to send her crawling back into bed.

AE HINES

PRAGUE

In what now seems a dream, you rouse me
from our bed and we set off to see the city
in darkness. Beneath the St. Charles Bridge,
a single dinghy slow dances against the hull
of a rusted-out barge. Fog. Distant bells.
A small clacking of birds. How long has it been:
that October sunrise glinting off the water,
a single swan dipping her neck in the mist?
Couples yet to stroll arm in arm, no shopkeepers
rattle to open their slanted steel doors. We stop
to take pictures atop the ancient city wall—both
of us frozen against a vacant fabric of new sky. Then,
the world re-peopled. Time, again, pulling
its relentless needle and thread.

AE HINES

LYING IN THE GRASS AT NIGHTFALL

There's a stout raccoon drowsing up
in my walnut tree, soft flesh folding over
a Y-shaped hammock of branches.
He's gorged on the neighbor's baby koi
whose keep was too shallow, a pond
my neighbor must drain and dredge, begin
anew. Nature is always teaching us things.
Twilight. A Tuesday. It bears repeating:
I am alive, plumbing the shadowy essence
of self, and this masked raider regards me
as I regard him, having crushed and swallowed
a dozen tiny suns. As he stretches and yawns,
a ripened drupe, a single dark orb, falls,
and like Newton's apple, thumps my unripe head.

AE HINES

SIGNAL FIRE

My gentle queries pile up
and hang on little blue clouds
in a towering one-sided text

with my newly adult son. I've
fallen in love with his one-word replies,
grown hooked on his ellipses, those

three blinking dots strobing left to right
which too often disappear with no message,
no new green bubble bearing his name,

no sturdy, *whoosh-whoosh, tap-tap*
vibration in my hand that has become
my substitute for proximity.

Is this what it means, now, to be in touch?
Across the jagged mountain of hours,
gray-white circles flash

like far-off fires, and every fortnight
a carrier pigeon, coos and teeters
in the soft flesh of my palm.

AE HINES

A GHOST IN
FLIGHT

MICHAEL BROOKS

2005

When the kid stumbled through the oaks onto his property, Bruce almost dropped his shovel. The kid followed Bruce's retriever down the hill toward the cabin, the dog's coat glowing golden in the sun. When the kid looked up and froze, Bruce felt a melting sensation, something like dry ice in his throat. He looked twice to be sure. But it wasn't Jonah.

"'Lo there," Bruce called. The kid stood in place like he'd been caught, which was strange. Because he didn't dress like a hoodlum, all the loose clothes and short-brimmed hats teenagers wore. In fact, he dressed a hell of a lot more like he was going on safari: nylon pants, a brimmed hat, and a bandana clinging cowboy-style to his neck. The kid glanced to the side, but Bruce beckoned him down the hill. And looking real self-conscious, he came.

The kid surveyed the cabin's eaves, the antlers mounted above the porch, and the south side of the yard, where beds of vegetables rose from wooden boxes. High chicken wire walled the boxes, some of which sported trellises made from quarter-inch conduit pipe and nylon netting. The kid glanced over at the chickens milling outside their coop, then at the blueberry bushes hugging the pole barn, the gravel driveway, and the three apple trees at the edge of the property.

Bruce took a good look at him. He was tall, had to be in high school. But his face held a softness, something that made him seem younger than his height. His eyes curved in the same round-almond shape as Jonah's but held a different hue.

"You lost, kid?" Bruce asked.

"Well, actually..." His nose wrinkled, perhaps at the scents of peat moss and compost rising from the boxed gardens. He fished a folded paper from his pocket and unfurled it. It was creased into quadrants, and when he held it upright, white sand spilled from its folds. He pointed to the corner of one quadrant. "I think I'm right here."

Inked across the paper were black whorls. Bruce peered closer. They were topography lines. "You know that doesn't work without a compass, right?" Bruce said.

"The Lake's my compass. It's always west."

"I see... Now, where on God's green earth did you get a topo map of Grand Mere?"

"Google," the kid mumbled.

"Noodle?"

"Google. It's a search engine."

Bruce glanced at the pole barn. "You know about engines?"

"It's a search engine. Like, on the Internet, you know? You type things in, and it finds them."

"What are you searching for?"

The kid's mouth hung open, as if hoping an answer would spring from his tongue. Jonah used to do that.

"I'm just giving you a hard time, kid. Name's Bruce. Bruce Kuipers." He held out his hand.

The kid nodded politely but didn't shake it. "Tyson Fischer."

"How old are you, Tyson?" Bruce asked, lowering his hand.

"Fifteen, but I'll be sixteen in August." The dog wove around the kid, sniffing his pants and licking his knuckles.

"Tolkien here seems to like you."

"You named him after the author?"

"Yeah," Bruce said, scraping a boot against the box to peel the dirt from its sole. Linda had named the dog, but Tyson's question surprised him. He didn't know kids still read. "So what are you doing in the woods?"

"I...I—sorry, I'm not, like, trespassing or anything. Just learning to survive."

"Aren't we all?" Bruce said with a grin. "Tell you what, I'll let you in on a secret. You want to survive? Get a shovel, use the shit life throws at you for compost, and plant a garden. That's all there is to it."

Tyson looked down at the boxed gardens. It was early June, and besides the lettuce and chard, only green shoots sprang from the soil, indistinguishable from one another. "What are you growing?"

"All kinds of veggies. In this box, tomatoes, peppers, eggplants, some basil..." And not knowing why, Bruce prattled on about compost and soil nitrates and mixing vermiculite in for a quick-draining base. Tyson nodded, his gaze snapping toward the trees every now and then while Bruce went on about Michigan's growing season for tomatoes and peppers and cucumbers until Tolkien lay down in the dirt yawned.

"I—I should probably go," Tyson said, glancing at the eight-point rack and then back at Bruce. "But thanks for all that." And before Bruce could say anything more, he pivoted and said, "So long!" over his shoulder, his hat and brown hair bouncing as he disappeared behind the wall of oaks from where he'd come.

■ ■ ■

Bruce opened the door to the pole barn that evening, and in the dark could just make out the rounded silhouettes of airplane parts. He flicked on the lights, and there was his bare Cessna, all cabin and fuselage, the ground littered with braces, ailerons, and the propeller. He made his way over the cracks in the concrete to the cockpit and entered. The buzzing from the barn's fluorescents dulled as he pulled the plane door closed, leaving only the sound of his exhalations.

A film of dust coated the dash, but he could still read the gauges. Altimeter: zero. Fuel: empty. Airspeed: zilch. He slid his feet to the pedals, curled his fingers around the steering yoke, and took a deep breath. He looked to the empty co-pilot seat, conjuring up the image of Jonah on the first day he'd taken his son airborne. Those brown, curious eyes scanning the counsel, mouth agape. The sky had held a color so rich, Jonah called it blueberry. They flew through the blueberry sky, the sun shimmering off rivers and inland lakes, turning them emerald.

"Look out the window, Jonah," Bruce said, as he had to his five-year old that day, the two of them skimming over the tapestry of green forests below. Beyond was a sliver of sand and the flat eternity of Lake Michigan, the sun sparkling across its swells.

The boy's swinging feet slowed as Bruce named the places the coastline protruded. There's South Haven, he said, And look! That river leads from Saugatuck to Kalamazoo. There's an old lumber town called Singapore buried beneath all that sand.

Jonah's headset looked enormous against his profile, and he breathed into the microphone, as quick as a hummingbird, as deep as a bellows.

"What'cha think of that, bud?" Bruce asked.

Jonah's white-blond head angled to the window, and he stared wide-eyed through its glass, Bruce witnessing what few others would have the chance to glimpse: flight from the sight of a boy.

Jonah grinned up at Bruce who clapped a hand on his shoulder and said, "Mommy's not gonna believe this, huh?"

A shadow leapt onto the nose of the plane. Lucky, the black cat who resided in the pole barn, stretched on her haunches and curled into a ball where the propeller should have been. And Bruce found himself once more in the dim barn, grounded, the seat empty beside him, the roof of his mouth dry from talking aloud. He swallowed, fumbled at the cabin door, and then angled away from the plane. He flicked the light switch, waiting for the cat to scamper into the starry night before closing the barn door.

The Big Dipper glowed overhead. Inside the house, Tolkien wagged his tail as Bruce scratched the dog behind the ears. He took his wristwatch from the nightstand. He never wore it during the day, when his hands fished into the loam of the earth, but at night, cold as a handcuff from the air-conditioning, it tethered him from the weightless feeling of the world between dreams.

He settled down to the swooshing sound of the sheets against his legs, the same sound ghosts sang when they haunted the living. Tolkien rested his chin on the bed and whimpered, and Bruce stretched out his hand and stroked the dog's muzzle. The watch's second hand bounced in the spaces between the numbers and dashes, around and around in its tiny orbit.

■ ■ ■

Bruce hacked at the broccoli stalk with the blade of his shovel. The summer heat had deformed the crown, its overall shape reminding him of the first brain scan he'd seen from the hospital. He thought it a sick joke. A mistake. A mix-up in the records. Faulty equipment. The incompetence of the staff. Of the doctor himself. A tumor? How could a seven-year-old have a brain tumor? He had refused to believe it, but had vomited nonetheless on the concrete steps in the parking garage. And now this: a twisted, deformed vegetable he sliced with steel and buried in a storm of brown earth. He strained and heaved and swore until he leaned against the handle panting.

"Are you okay?"

He whirled around. It was that kid, Tyson, his head tilted sideways, gangly arms at his sides. "Found a shovel," Tyson said, pinching a trowel by the hole in its handle. It swung like a pendulum.

"You might need a bigger one down the line," Bruce said.

Tyson pointed it at the raised garden bed and asked, "So how do I start one of those?"

Bruce wiped the sweat from his brow. "Depends what you want to grow."

"Not broccoli..." Tyson said, eyeing the plant.

Bruce took a deep breath, nodded, and explained the advantages of raised beds, how to start a compost pile, and why, this late in the season, transplants were a better bet than seeds. He barely heard his own words, transfixed by the leftward part in Tyson's hair, the same part Jonah had sported when he still had hair.

Bruce gestured toward the pole barn. "Might be a real shovel in there," he said. "Go on. Have a look."

Tyson disappeared into the barn, re-emerging moments later with a spade and wide eyes. "There's a plane in there!"

Tolkien barked, and Bruce tossed the dog a stick. "My old Cessna. A Skyhawk 172," he said.

"Could it run?"

"Oh sure. It'd be a big job though. I'd have to reattach the wings, probably overhaul the whole engine, oil the ailerons, figure out that propeller. The whole nine yards..."

He whirled around. It was that kid, Tyson, his head tilted sideways, gangly arms at his sides.

"How long would that take you think?"

"'Bout four months. Three if I hit it every day."

"What if you had help?"

"Oh? You're an experienced aircraft builder, Mr. Fischer?"

"No. But I'm a fast learner."

Bruce pressed the shovel in the dirt and leaned against it, taking a sideways glance at the broccoli stalk.

"C'mon, Bruce, let me help." Tyson said, almond eyes widening. "I'll even do for free, as a trade for all the gardening lessons."

■ ■ ■

Sawdust fountained onto the pole barn's floor. The smell of it dried Bruce's nostrils. "Your turn," he said. Tyson approached the miter saw, squinting to line up the blade and the crude pencil mark scratched over the 2x4. Tyson pushed the board to the fence and reached for the handle, glancing over his shoulder.

"I just pull the trigger and bring it down?"

"Cleanly," Bruce said with a nod.

He squeezed the trigger and his hands shot off the machine. "What's wrong?"

"The thing's having a seizure!"

Bruce grinned. "It's supposed to do that."

Tyson squeezed again, hovering the spinning blade over the board. He brought it down, the saw screaming through the wood, and then up again. "Crap..." he said, holding up an angled end.

"Push it flush against the fence with your other hand," Bruce said. Tyson heeled his hand against the board and triggered the saw to life. But he wasn't pushing hard enough.

Bruce sighed, stepping in and putting his left hand over Tyson's to steady the board. The kid's arm stiffened. Bruce nearly pulled back, but Tyson hadn't let go of the trigger. "Like this," Bruce said over saw's whine. "Push it that hard. Now bring her down."

Tyson started to, but his right arm shook.

The hell was wrong with this kid? Bruce wondered. The saw hovered over the wood, the plastic guard peeled back, blade whirling, each steel tooth catching the sixty-watt bulbs in the barn and ricocheting back their light. "Tyson, dammit, bring the saw down."

Bruce grabbed Tyson's right hand and forced the handle down. The kid's knuckles pressed into the concavity of Bruce's palm. The machine shook something awful—or was that Tyson?—shrieking through the 2x4 and showering their arms in sawdust when Bruce pulled up the handle.

The saw stopped.

"See?" Bruce said, taking his hands from Tyson's. "Clean break."

Tyson turned. His almond eyes were wide, his forehead clammy, his skin the color of chemotherapy. Bruce stepped backward, tripping over his feet, catching himself on a sawhorse. "Tyson? What's wrong?"

"I—I got sawdust in my eye," he said. Was he crying? He shivered out the door before Bruce could blink. Bruce crimped his fingers around the new-cut board and peered through the glass pane of the pole barn door. Tyson sat in the grass, Tolkien licking color back into the kid's face. Tyson's hands moved up and down the dog's sides, golden fur cresting in the spaces between his fingers. Bruce threw the board to the floor. It slapped the concrete and bounced before coming to a halt. He shouldn't have raised his voice, shouldn't have sworn. But really? What the hell just happened?

■ ■ ■

The shopping cart held all the things Bruce couldn't produce at home: milk, butter, bread, meat, soap, cheese, Motrin. He wheeled out of the frozen food aisle, ignoring the kids riding on the front of other carts and the popsicles for which Jonah would have begged.

"Bruce?"

He turned. Shirley Krauss stood by the refrigerators of cream cheese and hummus with a basket full of groceries.

"'Lo, Shirley," he said and then paused. "It's good to see you. How are things at the bakery?"

"Busy as usual. Lots of graduation cakes right now. I hired a new gal for the summer, and she's working out pretty well."

"That's good. And Mitchell?" Her son. Jonah's good buddy since kindergarten.

"He's headed to Western in the fall. On a hockey scholarship."

"That's great. Tell him I said congrats."

"How are you doing, Bruce?" She paused. "Out there?"

He supposed she meant Grand Mere, the woodsy dunes separated from the rest of Stevensville by a bridge over I-94.

"Just fine thanks."

"Alright. Well, if you ever need anything—"

"Thanks, Shirley."

She gave a nod and turned toward the tea and coffee aisle.

Shirley?" he called.

"Yes?"

"Listen, I got this kid that wanders on my property every now and then. Seems friendly, but I wondered if you knew anything about him. Says his name's Tyson."

"Tyson Fischer? Real sweet boy. Nothing to worry about there. Smart as a whip and quite the soccer player from what I hear."

"Fischer..."

"Yeah, his father's a big-wig at Whirlpool. You know, VP of sales or something like that."

"So he's well off?"

"Loaded. Has a brother too, who graduated this year. I made his cake."

"And his mother?"

Shirley pursed her lips. "You know this town, Bruce."

"Things are rocky with the couple?" Bruce asked.

"She left."

"Left?"

"Left him. Left Tyson. Left town. Met some doctor on the other side of the Lake, and, well..."

"Damn..."

"Yeah, shame too. Tyson's such a sweet kid." She switched the basket to her other hand. "You ever hear from Linda, Bruce?"

"I don't."

"I'm sorry about that. Well…" She looked around the store as though she had other places to be. "You hang in there, Bruce, okay?"

"Thanks, Shirley."

■ ■ ■

Bruce used his electric razor to give Jonah a crew cut while Linda jabbered at him about symmetry. "Aw, Jeez, Bruce," she said. "That's too short. He wanted GI Joe, not Nikita Khrushchev…" Bruce mumbled a few choice words while Jonah shifted in the kitchen chair and glanced sideways out the window.

"Straight ahead, co-pilot," Bruce said, taking the boy's chin in his thumb and the side of index finger and angling it forward. He pointed the razor at the refrigerator. "Eyes on that horizon line."

"Daddy…"

"I'm almost done, Jonah."

The cut would ease the technicians' job of pasting electrodes to Jonah's head. The razor sawed at Jonah's hair, blond tufts falling to his shoulders before littering the kitchen floor. It made Bruce queasy, bringing back memories of sheep shearing—the naked animals shivering in the early breezes.

Bruce held up a mirror, and Jonah smiled at the cue ball shape of his head, showing the pink gum of a missing front tooth while Linda swept the floor. "Time to load up the car, buddy. You ready?" Bruce asked.

Jonah knew nothing about white blood cell counts. He only knew that the doctors would make him sit still and prick him with needles. Sometimes, Bruce had to hold him in his lap, wrap his arms around the boy's squirming body, watch those needles break the skin on Jonah's arms and fingers, listen to the shrill of his son's screams.

Jonah's lip quivered when Bruce said again, in as gentle a voice as he could muster, that it was time to load up the car and not forget the Legos. Jonah bolted out the screen door, Linda shouting after him, her voice catching in her throat. She grabbed the chair to steady herself, and Bruce bounded out the door after him.

Jonah's bare feet kicked up a flurry of orange leaves as he fled into the trees, where he became shadow among the trunks, vanishing from sight. Bruce found him long minutes later, balled up and crying under an oak. He settled into the leafy bed beside his son. He whispered and hummed and rubbed his back until Jonah allowed Bruce to carry him home, his arms wrapped around his Bruce's neck, eyes holding that same, penetrating look Bruce had seen loading farm animals into wagons as a kid—a look gravid with trust.

■ ■ ■

Bruce rolled from the mattress, splashing cold water on his face in the bathroom and opening the bedroom closet. He yanked the pull chain for the overhead light and between two work shirts found the nightgown Linda had forgotten to take when she left. He peeled it from the wire hanger, about to click off the light when he glanced to the shelf. On it, a dusty box, and inside, an H&R Handi rifle, a first time hunter's gun. He'd purchased it while Jonah was in chemo, for when he recovered. Bruce killed the light and stumbled back to bed, Tolkien's tail thumping against the floor like a heartbeat. He lay back down and pressed Linda's nightgown over his nose and mouth, inhaling the last hints of perfume she'd worn in the years before cancer.

■ ■ ■

Bruce asked Tyson questions that set the kid's eyes in orbit and his fingers tapping. Like why he kept showing up and offering to help, and why he was so jumpy.

"Probably need pills or something," Tyson said.

"Nah, you need a father. No pill can fix that."

Tyson said nothing for a few seconds while Bruce poured water over a row of eggplants.

"Did you ever want a son?" Tyson asked.

"I have a son," Bruce said, so sharp he surprised himself.

Tyson's shoulders tightened, but he asked, "Where is he?"

"With his grandma and grandpa," Bruce said, having buried Jonah in the same plot as his parents.

Tyson leaned on the spade. "All summer? Do you not like him or something?"

Bruce looked away.

Bruce asked Tyson questions that set the kid's eyes in orbit and his fingers tapping. Like why he kept showing up and offering to help, and why he was so jumpy.

"How old is he?" Tyson asked.

Bruce squeezed the shovel's handle. How old? Did Bruce say eleven years, ninety days, and thirty-four minutes, Jonah's age when his heart stopped? Or did he say seventeen years, seventy-two days, and whatever godforsaken hour his watch would read had he nerve enough to wear it in the daytime?

"Seventeen."

"What's his name?"

"Jonah."

The weather vane creaked on top of the pole barn.

"I think we're all done for the day, Tyson." Bruce said. "I'll see you tomorrow."

■ ■ ■

With the propeller remounted, the Cessna transformed from a junkyard exoskeleton into a semi-believable aircraft. Bruce fitted a nut and bolt into place while Tyson droned on about hunting. "You can't just survive on plants in the winter. Gotta down a deer or two, right?"

Bruce grunted. "Want to hand me that socket wrench?"

Tyson eyed the toolbox.

"Thin metal thing with a rounded black end," Bruce said. "It's in there somewhere."

Tyson shifted the contents, and Lucky scurried away in the clattering.

"This thing?" Tyson asked. "Gosh. Looks just like the Neuralyzer."

"The what?"

"You know, from *Men in Black*?"

"Who's in black?"

"It's a flashy, pen-looking thing that makes people lose their memory."

Bruce blinked. "That's a thing nowadays?"

"No! Just in a movie. I wish..."

Bruce raised an eyebrow. "You're fifteen. What the hell could you wanna forget already?"

Tyson's mouth closed. His gaze zipped down to the socket wrench. "How's this thing work anyway?"

"Line it up over the bolt end, grip the shaft, pull to tighten, and then crank it back up and start over."

Tyson did, smiling at the sound of the rapid-fire clicking, his mouth slightly agape, the same expression Jonah had worn when learning something new. Jonah, Bruce thought, and before he knew what he was doing, he brushed Tyson's cheek with the backs of two fingers.

The kid recoiled. The socket wrench dropped to the concrete with a clang like a gunshot. Bruce tried to say something, but instead of words came a guttural consonant between a "j" and a "t" that hung in the rafters.

"I—I gotta go," Tyson said, and without another word, he was out the door.

■ ■ ■

Two weeks passed before Tyson showed up again. And even then, Bruce only saw his outline in the trees. The kid kept his distance, the way Lucky had when she first started haunting the pole barn. Bruce went about his work, pruning the gardens that Tyson had planted, rewinding reels of fishing line, carving wood figurines on the rocking chair, and setting rabbit snares at different parts of the yard. And finally, when he was cleaning and oiling his rifle on the porch, Tyson emerged from the trees and started talking to him, like nothing had happened. They resumed their work on the plane and the gardens, and a few afternoons later, Bruce brought out the rifle for a shooting lesson.

Through the lens of his aviator glasses, Bruce sighted down the Marlin's barrel at one of three Coke cans atop a dirt mound. The can caught the sunlight, making Bruce squint. In his peripheral vision, he saw Tyson beside him, arms crossed and fingers drumming over the skin of his elbows. Bruce cranked the lever, loading a round into the chamber and flicking the safety off.

"Now she's live." He inhaled, paused, squeezed.

The Coke can leapt skyward and rolled down the mound.

Tyson stayed silent for a second, then gave a two-syllabled, "Damn..."

Bruce levered the safety back on and extended the rifle to Tyson. "Your turn."

Tyson hesitated. The wind picked up, the leaves sounding like a waterfall, clouds barring the sunlight. Tyson took the rifle.

"Tuck it into your shoulder," Bruce said. "Kick's gonna be nasty if you don't."

Tyson pulled the rifle into himself, lined up the can with the peep sight, jimmied the lever down and up again to load a round, and switched off the safety. He inhaled. The gun rang, its muzzle jumping into the air, but the can stayed put.

"Dammit!" Tyson said, hunching forward and cradling his shoulder.

"Pull it closer," Bruce said. "The kick's not half as bad if it's close."

Tyson cocked the rifle again, aimed, and squeezed with the same result. He rolled his shirtsleeve back, a purple welt forming on his shoulder. The Marlin was too much for the kid. A smaller rifle would do the trick, and Bruce just so happened to have one on the top shelf of his closet collecting dust.

"Hold tight," Bruce said. He returned with a first-outfitter H&R Handi, a .223 Rem, the kind you had to drop bullets into one at a time and then thumb the hammer to load. The gun was still shiny. He'd filled his pockets with ammo. "Try this guy," Bruce said.

"That little pea shooter?"

"Might just fit with those string-bean arms."

Tyson mumbled something as Bruce thumbed the rounds into the back of the Handi and cocked the hammer. They exchanged rifles. The wind ceased, and, somewhere in the distance, Tolkien barked. Bruce nodded and sat on a tree stump to Tyson's left. Tyson sighted down the barrel at the Coke can, closed one eye, and fired. The shot missed.

"Lot less kick," he said, taking another round from Bruce. He pushed it into the Handi himself, cocking it and taking aim.

Tyson steadied his breathing, and his shaking hands stilled. As he prepared to fire, the sun broke through the clouds. It caught on the Coke can and across the barrel of the rifle. It backlit the kid, spilling over his rounded shoulders, turning his brown hair a golden blond. He took aim, closing the eye Bruce could see, holding his line of sight, standing as still as a corpse. In the silence, a cardinal sang, and breath, audible breath, escaped the boy's mouth. Bruce's stomach lurched. He sat up on the stump, about to call his son's name when the shot thundered from the rifle.

The can lurched sideways and fell, the sound of it bouncing down the dirt and harmonizing with the echo of the gun. The sun sank behind the clouds, the kid's hair becoming brown again, him turning to Bruce with those blueberry eyes shouting, "Bullseye! Clean kill! You see that, Bruce? Clean kill!"

All of Bruce shook, and something like bile rose in his throat. Whatever he'd seen seconds ago, there was only this: a stranger, not the son he'd raised, leaving handprints on Jonah's rifle, shouting over the clucking chickens and cooing birds and every sound of the cabin homestead, "Clean kill! Clean kill! Clean kill!"

"Go home," Bruce said, not with force, but he meant it. His hands squeezed the end of the Marlin.

"Bruce! I got it! Did you see that?"

"Leave," Bruce said, voice shaking. He stood from the stump to full height, still clutching the gun. "Do as I say."

Tyson blinked, lowered the Handi to the ground, and took a slow step backward. "Wha—What'd I do?"

"Just go!" Bruce shouted, and by the time he looked up, Tyson was nothing more than a silhouette, a boy-shaped shadow fading in the oaks, a ghost in flight. ■

PANTHEON+

Swan songs
of stars
harmonize into
a ruler
the one you would
fiddle with
on an elementary
school desk
wood or plastic
of varying
colors green
purple or
otherwise
as the teacher
expounds upon
nuances of sums
while in the
distance suns
lend definition
to everything
getting further
away from
everything

ALEX STARR

FURL

We once shared
a single space
with the orange
dahlia in the garden
of the Rijksmuseum
the caked cracks
in dabs of paint
depicting clouds
layered last
millennium
and the hands
that layered them
with futures
yet to unfurl
and all pasts

ALEX STARR

ETERNAL CYCLE: HANNA'S WORLD

after Stephane Wrembel's album Terre Des Hommes

Consider the cyclamen after it blooms / how its summer slumber resembles death / yellowed leaves dropping / as though they will never / again drink light / When Ravel composed *Pavane pour une infante défunte* / people wondered / who the child was / the sad story of her death / though Ravel wrote the title / simply for love / of the sound / So in English / we've named it / Pavane for a Dead Princess / There is no princess / no life / no death / no child I want / to name / Hanna / who steps legato / to the pianist's study of overlapping hands / sequins stitched in her sweater / hands crossing over pearled notes / *La fille n'a pas la fin* / Hanna / born from song / ready to rebloom / the girl alive / on a winter evening / dancing

JESSICA CONLEY

ETERNAL CYCLE: SORCIERE!

The concierge walks each row of each tier
at the Théâtre des Champs-Élysées, collecting
programs from the oor, marking chairs

to be reupholstered. As he moves on to the stage,
picking up the triangle beater left in haste,
he replays the afternoon performance,

Stravinsky's *Le Sacre du printemps*,
in his mind, gauging the moment the audience
began to moan, then stand, then scream, beat upon

the heads of those near in that rhythm
of Part II, scene ii, the circle of ballerinas stomping
in crescendo. Though it was not, he remembers,

until the *Glorification de l'élue*—the sonority
of inconstant time, accented slurs and pizzicato
heard barbaric—that the politician in the second row

bit his wife's ear. The concierge had stayed
for the nal movement—the center puppet-ballerina,
her arms' and neck's fatal grace, entranced him.

He had never seen, had never heard,
a woman dancing to her death. He did not turn,
could not leave, even as the audience shoved him,

tried to force him through the side doors.
Now, after his shift has ended, he walks home
along the riverbank, noticing how the boats pitch

in the pulse of the Seine, how his shoes knock
against the cobbled streets, how stark
the branches of forsythia wild, composing yellow.

JESSICA CONLEY

THE
JUDGE

ELAINE FOWLER PALENCIA

What was it, he would like to know, if it wasn't too much trouble for the universe to inform him, about banana bread and death?

Wearily, the Judge leaned over and picked up the wrapped loaf from his door mat, unwrapped it from its cellophone—yes, it was banana bread, the tenth loaf he'd received since Jennie died—and lobbed the damn thing into the surrounding trees.

A note was taped to the underside of the Saran wrap. *Sorry for your loss. My thoughts and prayers are with you. Call me if you need to talk. Aleda Bannerman.* Under her name, she'd written her phone number.

Christ Almighty. Another widow. Aleda lived on Green Briar Road, halfway around the lake from his cottage. Used to work at the florist's in the old IGA building. What he'd heard, she'd nagged Charlie to death.

He crumpled the note and wrapping and tossed them into the wood box by the door, then unlocked the door and stepped inside.

An odor of bacon lingered from the previous weekend, and mouse. Had he forgotten to clean the pan? He went in the kitchen.

Sure enough, there sat the skillet on the stove, mouse tracks and droppings speckling the quarter inch of bacon grease in the bottom.

Well, so the hell what?

In the living room, he opened the drapes on the sliding glass doors. Outside on the weathered deck, the two Adirondack chairs still sat facing the view. He and Jennie would sit there of an afternoon in good weather to watch the sun go down, he with his Knob Creek, she with her vodka and cran.

Maybe today he'd throw both chairs over the railing, enjoy hearing them splinter on the rocks below. No need for two chairs now. And one chair would reproach him just as much. Why had he come back here?

Habit. Stupidity. Because he didn't know what else to do with the weekend.

Before him, the wide body of water shifted and sparkled all the way to the necklace of hills that separated Watkins Lake from Blue Valley, where he and Jennie had lived most of their married life. In the middle of the lake, where the waning sunlight had laid down a track of gold like a long goodbye, a lone bass boat rocked. In it stood a man, casting.

The healing power of nature, my ass.

He pivoted away from the view, walked to the couch against the far wall, and lowered himself onto it, feeling a twinge in his bad knee. He took his cell phone out of his shirt pocket and set it on an end table, then picked up the remote and turned on the TV. *American Pickers* would do. As soon as it came on, he turned down the volume and closed his eyes. He was so tired. Tired in his bones. The weeks of sitting by her bed in the hospital. The nights lying on the couch afterward, staring into the dark, because he couldn't bear the emptiness of their king bed. Too tired to kill himself just now, but maybe later. He'd brought the pills.

Out on Sassafras Lane, the narrow gravel road that led through the forest to the cottage, a white van growled along.

"Crap road," said the driver, a man named Delray for the town he was conceived in on his parents' one and only Florida vacation. "You'd think a judge would have it paved. It's untelling how much money they make. Plus, they take all kinds of bribes, is what Chandler said. The whole court system is crooked."

The woman in the passenger seat flicked her cigarette out the window and said, "Now, just remember what I said: I'm not shooting anybody." Her name was Brenda.

"He's not any good to us shot," said Delray. "We're following Chandler's plan to the letter. Take him up to the cabin and call the number Chandler got hold of. I have it on my phone. The dude's a big deal; they'll pay the ransom. All you do is hold your gun on him." He snorted. "Judges are pussies. They dish it out but they can't take it." He'd made her practice with the gun earlier that week, even shooting cans out at the quarry.

"How do we know he'll be there?" Brenda asked.

"He's always there of a weekend, gets in about four on Friday afternoons. Chandler scoped him out. His wife died, so he'll be alone."

"I don't have nothing against judges in particular," said Brenda. "I mean, not like Chandler does." She waved a hand. "I mean, did. What kind of judge is he? Drug court?"

"Who cares? Shut up and let me think," said Delray. "This is going to be in and out. Quick. And truthfully, Chandler could, at times, go batshit. It'll work better without him."

The Judge dreamed he was walking in a gray central European city at twilight, like the ones he'd visited on the last world tour. He was hungry and tired. No one was around. He didn't know what city it was, had no money, didn't know the language. How could he get home? He searched his pockets for a passport, tickets. Nothing. He walked on. Where was Jennie? Oh, God, Jennie. Was she lost, too? How could he protect…

"Hey! Hey, wake up!"

Struggling up from sleep, as from deep in the ground, the Judge opened his eyes. Two people stood in front of him, somewhat camouflaged by N95 masks and plain ball caps: a wormy-looking young man—hardly more than a boy from what the Judge could see of him--in commercially ripped jeans, a gray windbreaker and scuffed running shoes, with a scrolly blue tattoo disfiguring one side of his face and neck, and a young woman—girl--similarly dressed, with spiked pink hair and very white skin with acne dots. Both carried Glocks. The girl had the Judge's phone in her other hand. The glass door to the deck was open. The boy's eyes looked like holes.

His shotgun was in his SUV, parked around back.

"Stand up," barked the man boy. "Let's go."

The Judge blinked at them. The boy would weigh one forty at most, the girl maybe one fifteen. "Go where?"

"You're not asking the questions!" the boy screamed. "Get up!" When he pointed the gun, he turned it on its side like a punk would, and barked at the girl, "Go open the front door." She hurried to do as he asked.

The Judge considered. Jennie wasn't there. She wasn't at risk. Whatever they were up to, they couldn't hurt her, no matter what they did to him. Nothing could hurt her now. So, what did he care? It didn't feel real, anyway, but more like a storyline on the tour. Still, his heart thudded and he'd started sweating.

He got up from the couch. "What do you want?"

"Hey," said the boy to the girl, "better look around. Don't know what this sumbitch might keep out here like some

Jennie wasn't there. She wasn't at risk. Whatever they were up to, they couldn't hurt her, no matter what they did to him. Nothing could hurt her now.

camera or something." When she hesitated, he yelled, "The bedrooms. Wherever!" He turned back to the Judge. "Get over by the door."

The Judge sat back down on the couch.

The boy smacked him upside the head with the flat of his hand. "What'd I tell you?"

"Are you," asked the Judge, "kidnapping me?" He slid off the couch and into a sitting position on the floor, all three hundred and fifty pounds of him. He crossed his legs, Indian style, and folded his arms.

"What the fuck? Get up!" said the boy.

"Make me."

"Brenda!"

She came flying out of the kitchen, eyes blazing. "Now he knows my name. Way to go, Delray." She stuck her gun in the waistband of her jeans.

Delray began to kick the Judge in the buttocks and back. Then he hit him in the center of the forehead with the butt of the gun, knocking the Judge's head back. "Get up, you fat bastard. Get on your feet," he said, a whining note creeping in.

"I would prefer not to," said the Judge. He wanted to add that it was something Jennie used to say, from some book she liked—was it Dickens?—but the little pissant didn't deserve to know anything about her.

Delray cocked his arm again.

"He can't walk if you knock him out," snapped Brenda.

"Why me?" asked the Judge, smearing blood off his face with a forearm. Something was stirring in him. Something he hadn't felt for a long time.

"Shoot him if he tries anything," said Delray, stuffing his weapon in the back of his waistband. He bent, put his arms around the Judge, and tried to lift him. Then he tried by pulling on the Judge's arms. Finally, he tried pushing the Judge over on his side—was he planning to roll him to the door?—but that didn't work either.

"You didn't say he was gi-normous," said Brenda.

"Shut up," said Delray.

It was growing dark outside. The Judge had planned to go down to the dock for supper—they did a good catfish dinner. Beyond that disappointment, by God, the old feeling had indeed arrived. What he and Danny used to call Mofo Mayhem.

He rolled onto his knees and lumbered upright.

"Smart man," said Delray, waving at the door with the Glock.

The Judge grabbed Delray's wrist, pulled the arm out straight and did a quick, vicious arm lock. As Delray's elbow joint exploded, he screamed and dropped the gun. The Judge hoisted Delray over his head, quick-marched to the deck, and threw him over. There was a muffled howl and thud as the boy hit the rocks fifteen feet below, followed by silence.

He turned to find the front door ajar and the girl gone. Outside, an engine started up, followed by crashing and a clash of gears. Through a window he saw her trying to turn a van in the narrow drive. She gave up and caromed off in a circle towards the lane, clipping the wood pile and flattening Jennie's Rose of Sharon bush.

The Judge went to the deck railing and looked down. Shadows had nearly swallowed the immobile figure. He closed all the doors and locked them. Then he found his cell phone where the girl had left it on the kitchen counter and called the authorities.

Very late that night, after all the hoohah was over and he was back at home in town, he called Danny—it had been a while—and told him.

"Naw, man. Are you serious?" Danny said after he stopped laughing. "These peckerwoods thought you were a real judge? That doesn't say much for our reputation."

"Think how long it's been," said the Judge.

"Yeah, bro, but we were the shit in our day," said Danny. "You were the best at taking a chair to the head. How many did The Twin Tackles break over your numbskull, anyway?"

The Judge chuckled. "I didn't keep count."

Each paused to remember the glory days of their tag team act for WWE, Jim "the Judge" Jameson and Danny "the Jury" Calhoun.

"So, the kid," said Danny. "He gonna to make it?"

"Maybe. Skull fractured pretty bad, some other broken bones. The girl's trying to say the whole thing was somebody else's idea, some guy that OD'd last week in Lewis County." What he didn't say was, right after he threw the boy over the railing, he'd felt the most beautiful, diamond-cut moment of rage and joy. Like some imbalance in the natural order had been corrected. Not so much now, though. Poor little bastard. And Jennie was still gone.

Danny said, "I'm really sorry about Jennie. How you getting along?"

"Day by day, bro," said the Judge, taking the bottle of pills out of his pants pocket and setting it carefully on the kitchen table. "Day by day." ■

AUTUMN ON THE TUCKASEGEE RIVER

Translucent white wisps
rise from the murky water,
ghosts of speckled trout
lured in by fly fishermen

who rise from the murky water
like ghosts of their younger selves
lured in by fly fisherman
dreaming of futures unseen.

These ghosts of their younger selves
chase the sun like these men chase trout
dreaming of futures unseen
fleeting hopes, catch & release.

They chase the sun like these men chase trout
exuding power that ends in failure
fleeting hopes, catch & release.
They return empty-handed

exuding power that ends in failure
but maybe that's the point;
they return empty-handed
because the trout don't belong to them

but maybe that's the point
that nothing belongs to us
because the trout don't belong to them.
We are intertwined, not owners;

nothing belongs to us,
not even the ghosts of speckled trout.
We are intertwined, not owners.
We're just translucent white wisps.

JESSICA CORY

ELEGY

Someday your father
will die of brain cancer
and you will have to
sort the stories.

You will need to buy
two houses: a shed
and a mansion—
the first for the time

you and your baby sister
hid in the beige bounty
of your mother's closet
and turned off the lights,

squeezed yourselves
into two tiny girl-balls
beneath her row
of blouses while

your father hit her
over the head with a bottle
of Wish-Bone salad dressing,
or set the kitchen on fire.

The shed would house
the gambling debts
and the nightly stumbles
from the fridge to the bed

the crooked trail
of potato chip crumbs
or translucent peanut skin
particles, disintegrating

like pencil shavings
in his wake. The shed
would hide his threadbare
pajamas and his curled out

penis from the unsnapped flap,
the Athlete's Foot between
his hammer toes, the worn
leather of his black slippers,

and the smoke rings that floated
through the house like small
ghosts, the shapeless stench
of old tobacco landing invisibly

everywhere. The mansion
would glisten with his collection
of Rolexes, his prized
Patek Philippe, giant bottles

of Johnnie Walker Red
and Black, Stolichnaya,
Nyquil, Benadryl, Valium,
the ricotta cheesecake

his "pretty secretary"
brought to his bedside

that Christmas he lay flat
in traction, their holiday

ease and laughter gurgling
through the halls as they
shared sips of Amaretto.
The mansion would burst

with mail-order steaks,
his Corvettes and Porsches,
the country club trophies,
the extraordinary amount

of money he offered my sister
to lose weight at college,
the last steps I saw him take
a year before he could no longer

walk—long night-strides from
the lounge chair at the hotel
pool to his water-view room
after yelling at me that my son

was too fat. The moon was full.
I was fifty-two, but I may as well
have been eight, crouched
with my sister in the dark

of my mother's closet—
her Lucite drawers
like a mausoleum
of underwear; the faded

red carpet dry ground
for the dead animal
pelts dripping from
her mink jacket.

CINDY MILWE

TWINNED FLESH

I see my old body
through the mottle
of stretch marks.

It is shy, afraid to speak
up in the shadow
of this mother-cover.

Twinned flesh,
no carapace—
the empty den

of my abdomen
frigid, dark, echoey
as an old bell tower.

CINDY MILWE

CONTRIBUTORS

Michael Brooks received his MFA from Pacific University and teaches writing classes at Hope College. His work has appeared or is forthcoming in *Redivider, Qu Literary Magazine, EcoTheo Review, Wayne Literary Review,* and *The Windhover.*

Jessica Conley teaches at The Steward School in Richmond, Virginia. She holds a BA in English, an MA in Secondary English Education, and an MFA in Poetry from Virginia Commonwealth University. She has been published in literary magazines such as *The Gordian Review, Glassworks Magazine, Common Ground Review,* and *2River.*

Jessica Cory teaches at Western Carolina University and is a PhD candidate specializing in Native American, African American, and environmental literature at the University of North Carolina, Greensboro. She is the editor of *Mountains Piled upon Mountains: Appalachian Nature Writing in the Anthropocene* (WVU Press, 2019) and the co-editor (with Laura Wright) of Appalachian Ecocriticism and the Paradox of Place (UGA Press, 2023). Her creative and scholarly writings have been published in the *North Carolina Literary Review, North Dakota Quarterly, Northern Appalachia Review,* and other fine publications. Originally from southeastern Ohio, she currently lives in Sylva, North Carolina.

Lauren Crawford holds an MFA in poetry from Southern Illinois University, Carbondale where she served as an associate editor for *Crab Orchard Review.* A native of Houston, Texas, she is the second-place winner of the 2020 Louisiana State Poetry Society Award from the National Federation of State Poetry Societies, and her poetry has either appeared or is forthcoming in *Poet Lore, The American Journal of Poetry, The Midwest Quarterly, The Worcester Review, The Spectacle* and elsewhere. Lauren currently teaches writing at the University of New Haven with her husband and is a reader for *Palette Poetry.* Follow her on Twitter @LaurenCraw4d

Carrie Green is the author of *Studies of Familiar Birds: Poems* (Able Muse Press, 2020). She earned her MFA at McNeese State University in Lake Charles, Louisiana, and has received grants from the Kentucky Foundation for Women, the Kentucky Arts Council, and the Louisiana Division of the Arts. Her poems have appeared in *American Life in Poetry, Verse Daily, Terrain, Poetry Northwest, DIAGRAM,* and many other journals. She lives in Lexington, Kentucky, and works as a librarian in a public library.

AE Hines's debut collection, *Any Dumb Animal,* received Honorable Mention in the North Carolina Poetry Society's 2022 Brockman-Campbell Book contest and was a daVinci Eye finalist for the Eric Hoffer Book award. His work has also recently appeared in *Alaska Quarterly Review, The Southern Review, Rhino, American Poetry Review, Poet Lore,The Greensboro Review, Ninth Letter, The Missouri Review, I-70 Review,* and *Tar River Poetry,* among other places. He resides in Charlotte, North Carolina and Medellín, Colombia. Find him online at www.aehines.net.

Jason Kyle Howard is the author of *A Few Honest Words: The Kentucky Roots of Popular Music* and co-author of *Something's Rising: Appalachians Fighting Mountaintop Removal.* His work has appeared in *The New York Times, The Atlantic, The New Republic, The Nation, Washington Monthly, Salon* and other publications. He directs the creative writing program at Berea College and serves on the faculty of Spalding University's Naslund-Mann Graduate School of Writing.

Jad Josey's work has appeared in *Ninth Letter, Glimmer Train, CutBank, Passages North,* and elsewhere. He has been nominated for the Pushcart Prize, Best of the Net, and Best Small Fictions, and his story, "It Finally Happened," was selected for inclusion in the Best Microfiction 2021 anthology. Josey is currently at work on a short story collection and a collection of poetry. Read more at www.jadjosey.com or reach out on Twitter @jadjosey.

Cindy Milwe is a writer and teacher who lives in Venice, California with her husband and three children. Her work has been published in many journals and magazines, including *5 AM, Alaska Quarterly Review, Poetry East, Poet Lore, The William and Mary Review, Flyway, Talking River Review,* and *The Georgetown Review,* among others. She also has poems in three anthologies: *Another City: Writing from Los Angeles* (City Lights, 2001); *Changing Harm to Harmony: The*

Bullies and Bystanders Project (Marin Poetry Center Press, 2015), and *Rumors, Secrets, & Lies* (Anhinga Press, 2022). Her first full-length collection, *Salvage*, was published last year by Finishing Line Press.

Mary Carroll Moore's short fiction and poetry has been published and/or won awards with *Fictive Dream, Quay, The Bellingham Review, Pitkin Review, Glimmer Train Press, The Airgonaut, Etched Onyx, Rappahannock Review, Santa Fe Writers,* and other publications. Her queer young adult novel, *Qualities of Light,* was nominated for the PEN/Faulkner Award, and her second novel, *A Woman's Guide to Search & Rescue,* was released in 2023.

An award-winning writer and freelance editor, **Elaine Fowler Palencia** grew up in Kentucky and Tennessee. A Phi Beta Kappa graduate of Vanderbilt University, she has authored six books of fiction; four poetry chapbooks; and a monograph, *The Literary Heritage of Hindman Settlement School.* She is the book review editor of *Pegasus,* the journal of the Kentucky State Poetry Society.

Alex Starr is a writer in the San Francisco Bay Area. His poems have been published in *Vallum: Contemporary Poetry, La Piccioletta Barca, Atlas & Alice, Black Sunflowers Poetry Press, Drunk Monkeys, Snapdragon Journal, The Literary Bohemian, Lunch Ticket, Zoetic Press, The Write Launch,* and *Meat for Tea: The Valley Review.* Starr's recognitions include the Dorothy Sugarman Prize in Poetry, George Harmon Coxe Award in Fiction, and Barnes Shakespeare Essay Prize from the Cornell University English Department. Starr holds a B.A. in Philosophy/English from Cornell and Oxford where he co-led the Mansfield College Poetry Society.

Dean Marshall Tuck is a writer living in North Carolina with his wife and daughters. His stories can be found in journals such as *The South Carolina Review, Epoch, Columbia Journal, Fugue,* and *The Florida Review.*

Joseph Vickery recently graduated from Oregon State University where he majored in creative writing. He is currently working on his MFA in writing at Lindenwood University. He has lived all over Tennessee, but now resides with his wife and kids in Nashville.

Lucas Warren lives with his family and a cat in Alberta, Canada. Unless he is travelling, he also writes there. His work has previously appeared in *CV2, The Antigonish Review,* and *Grain.*

www.ingramcontent.com/pod-product-compliance
Lightning Source LLC
Chambersburg PA
CBHW070605180626
46817CB00005B/2004